Welcome Back to Pleasant Hill

ELIZABETH C. KREMER

Pleasant Hill Press
Harrodsburg, Kentucky
1977

Original art work by Evalina K. Settle

First Printing
1977

Printed in the United States of America
by The Keystone Printery, Inc., Lexington, Kentucky

ii

I dedicate this book to my many friends who have shared their recipes with me.

"Let none abstain from food which they need; eat hearty and do the will of God."

Contents

Reflections on the Trustees' House

The Trustees' House—called the Trustees' Office by Pleasant Hill Shakers—was a place where members of the community met and did business with "the world" they had renounced. Begun in 1839 and completed in 1841, it was the center of trade and administrative activity. The "trading deacons" lived there, as well as the trustees and the office deaconesses who cared for the residents; it was a sort of separate "family" in itself.

Its one door is a sign of its unique function. All other buildings frequented by both men and women had a door for each sex. Here, where the Shakers met the world, both sexes might enter. For a brief period in Shaker history the world was allowed contact with the community *only* through the Office gate—which was believed to be guarded by an angel holding a flaming sword in one hand and a lighted torch in the other. Usually, however, the gate was a portal to hospitality for all. Elder Henry Blinn, recording his visit in 1873, noted his "hearty welcome" at the Office and the comfort of his stay with the community.

The Trustees' House exemplifies the paradox of Shaker life in several ways. It served for commerce with the world by those who had withdrawn from the world. Its architecture is simple and functional, yet it contains twin spiral staircases of unusual beauty. Historian Thomas D. Clark, who calls the stairs "an almost intoxicated spasm of romance," notes also the practical engineering sense involved in design and construction; the purpose of dual stairs was certainly practical from the Shaker view—the physical separation of men and women. These staircases are a beautiful achievement of harmony in their balanced separation; one feels the balance best by standing under one and looking up at the narrowing and perfected spiral that seems to symbolize the Shaker vision.

From the Trustees' House the Shakers sent gifts to those in need and maintained a lively business with the world. In the declining years of the community, it was for a short period a source of support: a "boarding house" where for a limited time "visitors could secure meals for forty or fifty cents, and daily board on equally as reasonable a rate."

When the Shaker community ended, the Trustees' House passed to other hands. In 1898 it went, with other property, to General John B. Castleman of Louisville. In later years it continued as a place of hospitality. In the 1920's and 30's, when Mrs. Nannie Jewell Embry had a popular tearoom in the East Family House, the Office was used for guests. It was a restaurant in the 1950's and early 60's owned by Mr. and Mrs. Robert Renfrew. The building was reopened as an inn and a restaurant in April 1968, as part of the Pleasant Hill restoration, where we try to recapture what we can of the Shaker concern with simplicity and craftsmanship. We hope Pleasant Hill's Shakers would be pleased to see the endurance of their crafted buildings and their spirit of welcome.

Guardian Angel

In Due Season

Pleasant Hill's journals reflect an agricultural community's involvement in the seasons. The scribes recount such events as the gathering of wild blackberries from the fields and river banks, of cherries from the cultivated orchards, and of vegetables from the tended gardens. They also note the work of preserving the fruits of the seasons for the lean months ahead.

Journal entries show close concern with environment. Writers record spring thaws and storms, delighting in early blossoms and fretting over sudden cold. They describe the pleasure of summer outings in good weather and the brethren's worries in time of drought. They comment on the beauty of an ice storm while registering concern with long periods of sub-zero weather.

In this book I've imitated a bit the pattern of those scribes whose careful script preserves an account of the Shakers' daily struggle to provide. Recipes are grouped by *Spring and Summer Gathering*; *Autumn Harvesting*; *Winter Cooking*; and *Food for All Seasons* (basic items on which the daily round depends and hospitality recipes for special occasions). And I've included quotations from the old journals—partly because I delight in them, but primarily in tribute to the conscientious and devout people who struggled with the elements, meticulously recorded their daily labor and rejoiced in the land.

Illustrations are based on Shaker "spirit drawings." These symbolic designs were derived from mystic visions given to believers as special tokens of love from Mother Ann. They were presents from the spiritual world to those who had renounced the earthly one. The drawings show how the Shakers saw eternity in terms of simple, natural images. Such things as apples and cherries, which were common fruits of the season, embodied eternal gifts of love and hope, which were permanent possessions of believers.

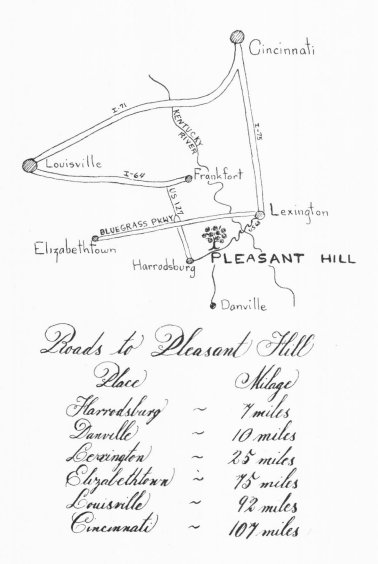

Roads to Pleasant Hill

Place		Milage
Harrodsburg	~	7 miles
Danville	~	10 miles
Lexington	~	25 miles
Elizabethtown	~	75 miles
Louisville	~	92 miles
Cincinnati	~	107 miles

Notes from the Author

Following the Shaker sense of seed-time and harvest, we use our garden produce and seasonal foods at the Trustees' House. Consequently, many recipes call for fresh vegetables; and in this day of rising food prices, I have given recipes which the home gardener can use for variety when garden produce is at peak season. Substitutions of canned or frozen vegetables may certainly be made, however, and I have indicated significant differences where necessary.

Some of the recipes in this book we have begun to use in the Daily Fare at Pleasant Hill since the publication of *We Make You Kindly Welcome*. Others are dishes which I just like and which are used by family and friends in Kentucky. Most are simple recipes and use ingredients you normally have around the house. Many can be prepared ahead of time and be refrigerated or frozen so that your dinner party can be a delight for you as well as for your guests. Some of the items—such as the pie crust and the country dressing—are repeats for your convenience, since they are basic to several recipes.

The following abbreviations are used:

T	=	tablespoon
C	=	cup
tsp	=	teaspoon
oz	=	ounce
pt	=	pint
qt	=	quart
lb	=	pound
gal	=	gallon

I wish to thank my daughters, Evalina K. Settle and Anna K. Reed, and my niece, Betty W. Morris, for their assistance in organizing this book; Jack Leonard and Jane Davis for their help and suggestions; and especially my kitchen and bakery staff at the Trustees' House on whom we all depend.

Spring and Summer Gathering

The Sisters turned out and set out turnips
                                    March 11, 1850

Mercury at 68. It has been showering since the 10th
during which time it has rained 1⅛ inches. Vegetation is
bursting forth and blooming like magic
                                    April 14, 1849

The Sisters set out strawberry vines after washing
                                    April 15, 1850

The Center and West Sisters trimmed off the thyme
and tansy in John's garden.
                                    May 1, 1850

Gathered currents and made 43 jars of preserves.
                                    June 12, 1849

Gathered blackberries at the cove spring and Varner fields
                                    July 7, 1849

There is a drouth prevailing to such an extent at present,
The pastures are litterally parched up... And yet the
sky is as clear and calm as if rain never came from there
and the weather moderate and cool for the season.
                                    August 5, 1856

Commenced gathering cucumbers for pickles.
                                    August 11, 1848

RAW VEGETABLE DIP

1 C mayonnaise
¼ C chili sauce
1½ to 2 tsp prepared
  horseradish

½ tsp grated onion
1 tsp whole mustard seeds,
  optional

Mix in order given, adding mustard seeds just before serving. Store in refrigerator until ready to use.

(This recipe is very good for dipping raw carrots, celery, fresh strips of yellow squash, and cauliflower, as well as chips and crackers.)

CURRY DIP

1 pt mayonnaise
2 to 4 T prepared horseradish,
  drained

¾ to 1 T curry powder

Start slowly, mixing and tasting for the flavor desired. Keeps indefinitely in refrigerator.

WATERMELON RIND PICKLES
A More Old Fashioned Kind

5 qts watermelon rind cubes
5 qts granulated sugar
2 C cider vinegar
4 qts water

2 tsp whole cloves
2 tsp whole allspice
4 to 6 sticks cinnamon
½ tsp ground ginger

Peel green rind from watermelon, leaving a little pink. Cut into about one inch cubes. (Can be cut into fancy shapes.) Measure the cubes then cover with brine (four tablespoons salt per one quart of water), and soak overnight. Pour off brine, wash in clear water and drain. Cover with fresh water and slowly cook until tender, about one hour. Drain again. Make pickling syrup of sugar, vinegar, and water. Tie spices in cloth bag and add to syrup. Bring all to boiling and pour over the watermelon cubes. Boil until watermelon cubes are clear, about one hour, and syrup is honey thick. Pack in sterilized jars. Store in cool place.

(If you wish a more tart watermelon pickle, replace one quart of water with one cup or more of vinegar. This is not the recipe served at the Trustees House because of the quantity needed.)

PICKLED OKRA

Okra, enough to fill 5 pt jars
5 halves small hot red peppers
5 half-cloves garlic
1 qt cider vinegar

½ C water
7 T salt
½ T celery seed
½ T mustard seed

Gather only the very young fresh okra when you are ready to pickle. Wash and allow to dry. Pack okra in sterilized pint jars. Into each jar put one-half red pepper and one-half garlic clove. Bring vinegar, water, salt, celery seed and mustard seed to a boil and pour over okra. Fill jars to top. Store in a cool dark place for several weeks before using.

ZUCCHINI PICKLES

6 to 10 medium onions, very
  thinly sliced
5 lbs of tender small zucchini,
  about 4 qts, sliced about ¼
  inch thick. Do not peel.
1 qt distilled white vinegar

2 C granulated sugar
¼ C salt
2 tsp celery seed
2 tsp ground tumeric
1 tsp dry mustard

Bring vinegar, sugar, salt, celery seed, tumeric and dry mustard to a boil. Pour hot liquid over zucchini and onions; let stand one hour, stirring occasionally. Bring to a boil; simmer three minutes. Continue simmering while quickly filling one hot sterilized jar at a time. Fill to within one-eighth inch from the top, making sure vinegar solution covers the vegetables. Seal each jar at once. Makes eight pints.

4

WATERMELON HALF WITH FRESH FRUIT

Watermelon, honeydew, cantaloupe, or other local melons, strawberries, raspberries, peaches, blueberries, or other fresh fruit.

Slice in half lengthwise, a fully-ripe watermelon. Scoop out reddest fruit with a small fruit scoop. Place balls in large bowl. With spoon scrape rough edges left in rind and discard. From other melons scoop out small balls. Cut fresh fruit into cubes of desired size. Add this to melon balls. Gently mix. Return to hollowed-out watermelon. Decorate with mint leaves. This should be made early in the day before serving and stored in the refrigerator until well chilled.

(If you do not have a small fruit scoop, melon and other fruits may be cut in small cubes. Any type of fresh fruit can be added to the melon balls. The small round watermelons, such as Dixie Queen or Crimson Sweet, are best for an attractive dish on your buffet table. When you use the smaller melon slice across in the center instead of lengthwise.)

ICED TEA WITH FRUIT JUICES

5 tea bags	1 six oz can frozen orange
4 C boiling water	juice
4 C cold water	juice of 3 lemons
2¼ C pineapple juice	1 C granulated sugar or less

Steep bags in boiling water for ten minutes. Take out tea bags and add cold water. Add pineapple juice, orange juice, lemon juice and sugar. Stir well and serve over ice cubes. Makes about three quarts.

(This will keep well in the refrigerator and is better if left to blend a while.)

5

COLD SQUASH SOUP

½ C onion, chopped
1 stalk celery, chopped
1 carrot, chopped
¼ C butter
4 C yellow summer squash,
  peeled and diced

1 medium potato, peeled
  and diced
1 qt beef stock or 4 boullion
  cubes and 1 qt of water
¾ C cream
salt and pepper to taste

Sauté onion, celery, and carrot in butter until soft, but not brown. Add squash and potato to beef stock, along with sautéed vegetables. Cook until squash and potato are tender. Strain, saving liquid. Force vegetables through sieve. Combine with liquid and mix in cream slowly. Season and chill. When serving cold, if butter rises to top, whirl a short time in blender before serving. Serves six.

(Cold soup is very refreshing on a hot summer day.)

 BISQUE OF GARDEN PEA

3 C fresh peas, or frozen
2 C water
pinch of salt
¼ C onions, chopped

3 T butter
3 T all purpose flour
3 C milk or half-and-half
salt and red pepper to taste

Cook fresh peas in water with pinch of salt until tender or according to directions on box of frozen peas. Cool slightly. Put peas, liquid and onions in electric blender, blend until smooth. In large sauce pan melt butter and stir in flour until smooth and bubbly. Remove from heat and stir in milk slowly. Return to low heat stirring constantly and cook until sauce thickens. Add pureed pea mixture and stir until blended. Season to taste with red pepper and salt. Chill until ready to serve. Garnish with chopped mint leaves.

(When those peas start coming in from the garden this is a delicious way to add variety to your menu.)

ZUCCHINI SOUP

scrubbed and
_ed
_ns, chopped
_utter

½ tsp garlic, chopped
1 tsp curry powder
½ C water
2 C chicken broth

Melt butter and sauté zucchini and onions slowly. Add curry powder, garlic and water to sautéed mixture. Cook, stirring often, until zucchini becomes soft. Cool slightly and pour in electric blender. Blend until smooth. Mix zucchini mixture with chicken broth. Season with salt and pepper to taste. Serve hot or cold.

(It is not necessary to peel very young zucchini,)

ICED POTATO SOUP

1 medium onion or 3 small
  leeks, chopped
2 T butter
6 medium old potatoes, peeled
  and chopped

4 C chicken broth
1 T salt
1½ to 2 C cream
red pepper or tabasco

Sauté onion in butter. Cook potatoes in chicken broth until tender. Add onion and butter to potatoes. Season with salt. Cool slightly before placing in electric blender. (Can be put through a sieve if a blender is not available.) Blend soup in small amounts to prevent overflow. Chill. When ready to serve add cream. Season with red pepper or tabasco and taste for more salt. If served hot, heat soup and add warm cream.

(Keep in mind, the next time you buy whole chickens, to freeze the uncooked necks and backs. When you have time, make your own stock from scrap chicken, water to cover, celery leaves, parsley, salt and pepper and store in freezer or refrigerator for just such recipes.)

7

THIN FRENCH DRESSING

6 T oil
2 T vinegar
¼ tsp salt
sliver of onion

2 tsp lemon juice
1 tsp granulated sugar
¼ tsp paprika

Put all ingredients in dressing bottle and shake well before using.

(This is a good basic thin dressing and will keep indefinitely in the refrigerator.)

BLUE CHEESE DRESSING

1¼ lb blue cheese, crumbled
1 large can evaporated milk
¼ C lemon juice

¼ C thin french dressing
2 qts mayonnaise

Beat all ingredients together until light and smooth. Put in a jar. Store in refrigerator.

(This is a large amount but will keep for weeks. A thin blue cheese dressing was in my first cookbook. We now use this one at the Trustees' House.)

COUNTRY DRESSING

1 tsp dry mustard
2 T granulated sugar
¼ tsp salt
2 T all purpose flour

½ C cold water
2 egg yolks
¼ C vinegar
2 T butter

Dissolve mustard, sugar, salt and flour in water. Beat eggs and vinegar in top of double boiler. Add the dissolved ingredients. Cook and stir the dressing over boiling water until thick and smooth. Stir in butter.

8

VIOLET VINEGAR

4 C violets, blossoms only   4 C white vinegar

Pack jar with violets and pour on the vinegar. Sit jar in sunny window until violets bleach out, four to five days. Strain. This can be used for an oil and vinegar dressing for garden salads (do not use olive oil), or mix one-half cup mayonnaise and one teaspoon granulated sugar and thin with violet vinegar. Use on salad greens.

(Pleasant Hill's grassy acres are a'bloom with violets in the spring and this recipe makes good use of these lovely blossoms.)

Mother Lucy's table of fruit

TOMATO ASPIC

1 envelope unflavored gelatin   2 tsp lemon juice
½ C cold tomato juice   salt to taste
1½ C hot tomato juice,   dash tabasco
   boiling point

Sprinkle gelatin over the cold tomato juice and stir until gelatin melts. Pour hot tomato juice into dissolved gelatin mixture and stir. Add lemon juice and seasonings. Pour in mold or individual molds that have been rinsed in cold water. Chill until firm. Unmold and serve on crisp lettuce leaves. Makes five small molds.

(You may add chopped or sliced olives or chopped celery to the aspic when it is cool before it jells. Cream cheese or grated cheddar cheese rolled into a small ball is also a nice addition to the aspic when it begins to jell.)

MARSHMALLOW SALAD

⅛ tsp dry mustard
4 egg yolks
½ C milk
juice of one lemon
salt to taste
1 C miniature marshmallows

1 C pecans, slightly chopped
4 to 6 slices drained pineapple,
  cut in small chunks
½ lb red or white grapes sliced
  in half with seeds removed
1 C heavy cream

Cook mustard, egg yolks, milk and lemon juice in double boiler until it thickens. Stir in salt to taste. Chill. Fold in marshmallows, pecans, pineapple chunks, and grapes. Whip cream until stiff and fold in last. Let stand in refrigerator several hours or overnight. Serve on crisp lettuce leaf.

SWEET CABBAGE SALAD

2 qts cabbage, shredded
1 large carrot, grated
1½ tsp onion, grated
2 stalks of celery, finely chopped

salt and pepper to taste
2 T granulated sugar
¾ C salad dressing
2 T sweet pickle relish

Toss vegetables together. Season with salt and pepper to taste. Sprinkle sugar over slaw and toss again. Mix salad dressing and pickle relish. Add dressing mixture to slaw. Stir. Chill until ready to use.

(This is a dry slaw. If you prefer, add more salad dressing. For an attractive way to serve slaw, slice stem at base of cabbage head so that head will sit firmly in platter. Hollow out cabbage head for slaw, but leave an attractive curl of outer leaves. Fill these leaves with sweet cabbage salad, or with Shakertown Cole Slaw. See We Make You Kindly Welcome, *page 18.)*

FROZEN FRUIT SALAD

1 pt heavy cream
1 C miniature marshmallows
1 C pecans, slightly chopped

2 C (#303 can) fruit cocktail, drained
¾ C country dressing, page 8

Whip cream until stiff. Mix together country dressing, marshmallows, pecans and fruit cocktail. Stir lightly. Fold whipped cream into fruit mixture. Put in mold and freeze overnight. Serve on lettuce leaf. Top with dab of mayonnaise. Garnish with mint leaves.

(This recipe is made with canned fruit but is very cooling on a summer day. Seedless grapes can also be added.)

POTATO SALAD

6 medium potatoes
2 T thin french dressing, page 8
1 T onions, chopped
¼ C celery, chopped
1 tsp green pepper, chopped

1 egg, hard boiled and chopped, optional
1 T pickle relish
½ C mayonnaise
salt and pepper

Cook potatoes in skins. When tender, drain and cool slightly. Peel and dice potatoes. Add french dressing and toss. Let stand about one hour. Add onions, celery, green peppers, egg and relish. Mix well. Stir in salt and pepper to taste. Add mayonnaise. Serve at room temperature or chill. Makes one quart.

(Amount of mayonnaise varies according to taste; add more if preferred.)

ROAST LAMB

Put one leg of lamb in a roaster. Place slices of one lemon and one onion on top of meat. Fill roaster with enough water to come halfway up on the meat. Cover and roast at 325⁰ for 35 minutes per pound.

LAMB SAUCE

½ C chili sauce
½ C mint jelly
1 T worcestershire sauce

1 T prepared horseradish
  mustard
1 pt of drippings from lamb
  roast

Mix ingredients in sauce pan and simmer for 10 minutes. Serve hot with lamb.

(This sauce is also very tasty on roast beef.)

MINT SAUCE

4 T chopped mint leaves
2 T granulated sugar

½ C cider vinegar

Pour vinegar over sugar. When dissolved add mint and sit in warm place for one hour or more before serving.

(These sauces are very different. Serve both of them and let your guests choose their favorite.)

FROG LEGS

12 frog legs
1 C all purpose flour
salt and pepper

2 eggs
¼ C milk

If frozen, thaw frog legs. Salt and pepper. Beat together eggs and milk. Dip frog legs in batter and then flour. Dip and flour again. Fill heavy skillet one-half inch up side with grease. Heat. Fry until golden brown and tender. Serve hot.

TUNA SPINACH CASSEROLE

1½ C spinach, chopped, or
   1 - 10 oz package frozen
   chopped spinach
1 - 6½ oz can flaked tuna,
   drained
⅓ C fine bread crumbs

1 T lemon juice
2 T grated parmesan cheese
¼ tsp salt
½ C mayonnaise
dash of pepper

Cook and drain spinach. Mix all ingredients folding in mayonnaise last. Spoon into individual scallop shells or nine-inch pie pan. Sprinkle with additional cheese. Bake at 350° for 20 minutes. Serve immediately. Makes four large servings.

TOMATO OKRA CASSEROLE

6 T onions, chopped
2 T bacon grease
1 lb okra, sliced
1 qt tomatoes, peeled and
   cooked, or canned
¼ tsp curry powder

½ tsp paprika
1 T sugar
1½ tsp salt
¼ tsp red pepper
2½ T parmesan cheese
8 butter crackers, crumbled

Sauté onions in bacon grease. Add okra and cook until tender. Add tomatoes and seasoning. Pour in greased casserole dish. Top with cheese then cracker crumbs. Bake at 350° for 35 minutes. Serves about 12.

STEW FRIED CORN

1½ C fresh corn, cut from cob or,
   1 - 10 oz box of frozen corn
1 T bacon grease
1 tsp granulated sugar

¾ tsp salt
⅛ tsp pepper
¼ C hot water
4 T butter

Melt bacon grease in skillet. Add corn, sprinkle with sugar, salt and pepper. Pour in hot water and break butter in small bits over corn. Cook about five to ten minutes. Serve hot.

SPINACH SQUARES

1½ C spinach, chopped or
   1 - 10 oz package chopped
   frozen spinach
½ C butter
⅓ C flour

1 tsp baking powder
8 oz brick cheese, diced
1 lb cottage cheese
6 eggs, beaten

Barely cook spinach if fresh. If using frozen, just thaw. Drain well. Melt butter. Sift flour and baking powder into butter. Stir well. Add spinach and diced brick cheese. Stir in cottage cheese. Beat eggs well and stir into spinach mixture. Pour into greased and floured 9 x 13 inch baking dish. Bake at 350° for 45 minutes to one hour.

(As a canape this is excellent, also delicious served as a vegetable dish at dinner. May be eaten hot or at room temperature.)

Lamb

ASPARAGUS CASSEROLE

2 C asparagus, if fresh, cook
½ C juice from asparagus
1 can mushroom soup

24 butter crackers, crumbled
½ C butter, melted

Butter a one and one-half quart casserole dish. Layer one-third of crackers and place asparagus on top. Mix asparagus juice with soup and pour over asparagus. Top with remaining crackers and melted butter. Bake at 325° for 30 minutes.

(For a little different taste, one-half cup of grated cheddar cheese, or one six-ounce jar of cheese spread can be added to soup before mixing. This is similar to broccoli casserole.)

BAKED FRESH TOMATOES

fresh tomatoes (desired number)   tarragon leaves
butter   parmesan cheese
salt and pepper

Remove stem from tomatoes and hollow a little. Place in shallow baking dish. Add a dab of butter and salt to each tomato. Top with parmesan cheese and tarragon leaves. Bake at 300° until just tender, not mushy.

BROWN SUGAR BAKED BEANS

2 large cans pork and beans   4 T brown sugar
  (31 ozs each)   2 tsp prepared mustard
2 T onion, chopped   1 C catsup

Mix all ingredients together in a two and one-half quart greased casserole dish. Place four strips of uncooked bacon on top. Bake at 350° for about one and one-half hours. Serves 10 to 12.

BROCCOLI CASSEROLE

2 C cut broccoli or 1 - 10 oz   4 T butter
  package, frozen   12 butter crackers, crumbled
¼ lb Velveeta cheese

Cook and drain broccoli. Melt cheese with half of butter. Mix with broccoli. Place in greased baking dish. Melt remaining butter and mix with crumbled crackers. Sprinkle crumbs on top of casserole dish. Bake at 350° for about 20 minutes. Serves three or four.

(This casserole can be made the day before using and refrigerated until needed. Add cracker crumbs just before baking.)

LEMON GLAZED CARROTS

1 qt tiny fresh carrots scraped
   and boiled until tender
2 tsp lemon juice

2 T light brown sugar
⅓ C granulated sugar
2 T butter

Place drained carrots in a greased baking dish. Combine sugars and sprinkle over carrots. Add lemon juice, dot with butter and bake at 450⁰ about 20 minutes.

(At Shakertown we use canned tiny Belgian carrots when fresh are unavailable. Commercially canned sliced carrots are equally good.)

CREAMED PEAS AND POTATOES

2 C early June peas (fresh,
   frozen, or canned)
6 tiny potatoes
½ pt heavy cream

1 T all purpose flour
a little water
dash of red pepper
1 tsp salt

Cook peas and potatoes separately. Drain. Combine vegetables in pan. Pour in cream. Make paste of flour and a little water. Stir into vegetables and cook until slightly thickened. Stir in butter. Add seasoning to taste. Serves six to eight.

FRESH BERRY MUFFINS

2 C blackberries, mulberries, or   ½ tsp salt
   blueberries   ¼ C butter
2 C flour, unsifted   1 egg, beaten
¾ C granulated sugar   1 C milk
3 tsp baking powder

Sift together flour, sugar, baking powder and salt in large bowl. Cut butter into flour mixture with a pastry cutter until butter is size of small peas. Beat egg and milk together. Add egg mixture all at once to flour mixture. Stir with fork until dry ingredients are moist. Batter will be lumpy. Add berries of your choice and quickly stir until blended. Fill well-greased muffin tins halfway full. Bake at 400⁰ for about 25 minutes. Makes 20 muffins. Freezes well.

(When gathering berries, freeze without washing. When ready to use dip quickly in water and remove stems. Use immediately before berries become mushy. If berries are too tart toss lightly in a little sugar before adding to muffins. If berries are not available fill muffin cups with small amount of batter and place two teaspoons jelly or preserves in cups and top with more batter.)

STRAWBERRY PRESERVES

1 qt stemmed and washed   1 qt granulated sugar
   strawberries   1 T lemon juice

Place sugar and strawberries in alternate layers in a kettle. Cover. Let stand overnight. In the morning stir to blend. Place over heat, stirring occasionally, and bring to a boil. Cook 15 minutes, stirring constantly to prevent sticking and boiling over. Remove from heat and add lemon juice. Cover with cheesecloth until next morning. Bring to a boil. Skim off foam with spoon. Place in sterilized jars and seal with parafin.

CINNAMON BREAD

2 C all purpose flour, sifted   1 C granulated sugar
½ tsp baking soda   2 eggs
1 tsp baking powder   1 C buttermilk
½ tsp salt   1 tsp vanilla
¼ C shortening

Preheat over to 350⁰. Sift together flour, soda, baking powder and salt. Set aside. Cream shortening. Add sugar and blend well. Beat until light. Add eggs beating until light and fluffy. Add flour mixture alternately with buttermilk. Mix well after each addition. Add vanilla. Mix until well blended.

2 T granulated sugar   1 T cinnamon

Combine sugar and cinnamon. Spoon half of batter into 9 x 5 x 3 inch well-greased loaf pan. Sprinkle three-fourths cinnamon sugar mixture on batter. Cover with remaining batter, top with remaining cinnamon mixture. Bake 50 to 60 minutes or until done. Cool completely before slicing. Wrap in plastic wrap until ready to serve.

(This may be baked in a ring mold pan and glazed .)

Bread Plant

HOT CROSS BUNS

It was a custom in medieval England to sell these little buns after church services on Good Friday to break the fast. The cry of "One-a-penny, two-a-penny, Hot Cross Buns," could be heard in all the towns and villages.

1 T yeast	1 egg, beaten
¼ C water, lukewarm	½ C raisins, seedless
1 C milk	½ tsp cinnamon
½ C granulated sugar	3 to 3½ C all purpose flour
½ C shortening	¾ tsp salt

Scald milk with sugar and shortening, then cool to lukewarm. Soften yeast in the lukewarm water. Sift together flour, salt and cinnamon. To milk mixture add softened yeast, beaten egg, raisins and flour mixture. Knead lightly in bowl, cover and let rise in warm place until doubled in bulk. Knead again on a floured surface. Shape into two-inch balls and place one inch apart on greased baking pan. Push down lightly with thumb to flatten slightly so bun will not be too high. If desired, snip a cross on top with greased scissors. Let rise until very light (doubled in bulk). Brush with beaten egg and bake for about 20 minutes at 375°. When cooled, fill in cross with icing. (See below.) Makes about 20 to 24 buns.

ICING FOR HOT CROSS BUNS

powdered sugar	hot water

Mix ingredients well. This mixture should be stiff. After buns have cooled on racks fill in crosses with small amount of icing.

(If you freeze the buns, heat them and ice them before serving.)

CHAN TORTE

7 egg whites
2 C granulated sugar
1 T cider vinegar
1 tsp vanilla

1½ qt strawberries, sliced
    and sugared
1 pt heavy cream

Beat at high speed egg whites, sugar, vinegar and vanilla until mixture is stiff and shiny. Line two eight-inch cake pans with oiled brown paper. Pour half of mixture into each pan. Spread to edge. Bake about one hour at 275⁰. Cool on rack. When cool remove pan and paper. Before assembling torte, whip cream until stiff. Do not assemble until ready to serve. Place first meringue layer on serving platter. Put one-third of whipped cream on shell and smooth out. Top with one-half of fruit. Place second layer of meringue on top of fruit. Put remaining fruit on top and cover with remaining cream. Decorate with a few berries. Serves about ten.

(This is equally good with fresh peaches.)

FRESH CHERRY PIE

3 heaping cups fresh cherries,
    washed and pitted
1 C granulated sugar

¼ C all purpose flour
1 T butter

Sugar cherries and let sit 24 hours in refrigerator, tossing occasionally. Line eight inch pie pan with uncooked crust and have top crust available. Sprinkle flour over cherries and mix well. Pour into pie shell. Dot with butter. Place top crust on pie and seal edges. With sharp knife cut slits in top. Bake at 425⁰ for 30 to 35 minutes. Juice will bubble through slits. Serve warm.

(This recipe may be used for blackberries, mulberries, strawberries, or gooseberries, but omit flavoring. If berries are very tart increase sugar. If berries are not tart enough a small amount of lemon juice may be added.)

CRUST FOR ONE PIE

1 C all purpose flour   ⅓ C plus 2 T shortening
½ tsp salt   2 T cold water

Mix flour and salt. Cut shortening into flour with pastry cutter until shortening forms very small balls. Sprinkle in water, a tablespoon at a time, while mixing lightly with a fork until the flour is moistened. Mix with hands into a ball that cleans the bowl. Do not overwork the dough. Roll out on floured board and place in pie pan.

(The less you handle dough, the better; handling toughens it. A good crust must be crisp, even at the risk of being a bit crumbly. Sometimes a tougher pie crust looks better, but this is one case where you must choose between appearance and taste.)

CYNTHIANA STRAWBERRY SHORT CAKE

Double recipe for Crust for One Pie so that you can make two pie crusts. Roll out one-fourth inch thick (or a little thicker than for one pie). Cut two eight-inch circles of crust, place on cookie sheet and prick with fork. Bake at 475° for eight to ten minutes. Place on serving plate and cover with strawberries and a small portion of icing, see below. Top with second crust and more sweetened strawberries. Pour plain white icing over top and allow to drip down sides.

PLAIN WHITE ICING

1 C granulated sugar   1 egg white, beaten until soft
½ C cold water   peaks form

Cook sugar and water until it hairs (230° on candy thermometer). Pour sugar mixture very slowly over egg white, beating all the while, until it mounds slightly.

(Have everything ready but do not assemble until just before serving. After beating, the icing will hold for about an hour.)

KENTUCKY PIE

1 unbaked pie crust
¼ C butter
1 C granulated sugar
3 eggs, beaten
¾ C white corn syrup

¼ tsp salt
1 tsp vanilla
½ C chocolate morsels
½ C chopped nuts
2 T bourbon

Cream butter and add sugar gradually. Add beaten eggs, syrup, salt and vanilla. Add chocolate morsels, nuts, and bourbon. Stir until well mixed. Pour into pie crust and bake at 375⁰ for 40 to 50 minutes. If crust browns rapidly, cover with foil or brown paper. Rewarm to serve. Serves seven or eight.

(This pie has become a tradition at Pleasant Hill's annual Derby Brunch.)

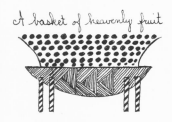

A basket of heavenly fruit

RHUBARB STRAWBERRY COBBLER

½ C all purpose flour
3 C granulated sugar
1 tsp salt
6 C rhubarb, sliced

2 C strawberries, sliced once
   if large
4 T butter
1 T lemon juice

Butter lightly 9 x 13 inch pan. Combine flour, sugar and salt. Sprinkle over rhubarb and strawberries, and toss well. Heap mixture into greased pan and spread. Sprinkle with lemon juice and dot with butter. Top with pie crust; prick crust or cut slits in it. Bake at 450⁰ for one hour.

(This may be served with a dip of vanilla ice cream. If you have a great deal of rhubarb from your garden, wash and slice, place in plastic bags in the freezer.)

22

BROWN SUGAR SQUARES

2 C brown sugar, firmly packed 1½ tsp baking powder
½ C butter   ½ tsp salt
3 eggs   1 tsp vanilla
1½ C all purpose flour   1 C nuts, optional

Mix softened butter with sugar. Blend in eggs. Add flour, baking powder, salt and vanilla. Beat until smooth. Stir in nuts if desired. Spread batter into 9 x 13 greased pan. Bake at 350⁰ for about 30 minutes. Score and when cool cut in squares. Makes about three dozen.

Bowl of Fruit

CHOCOLATE CHIP BROWNIES

1 C plus 2 T butter   2 eggs
1 tsp baking soda   ¾ C brown sugar
1 tsp salt   ¾ C granulated sugar
2¼ C all purpose flour   1 tsp vanilla
           1 - 12 oz package real chocolate morsels

Put butter in 9 x 13 inch pan and place in oven while preheating to 375⁰. When pan is hot and butter starts to melt, remove from oven and let sit until butter is completely melted. Be sure not to leave butter too long in oven as it should not bubble or froth. Tilt pan to coat bottom and sides and when butter is cool pour from pan into mixing bowl and add sugars and mix. Beat in eggs and vanilla. Add flour, salt and soda and mix well. Add chocolate morsels and pour back into baking pan in which butter was melted. Bake at 375⁰ about 30 minutes, or when center is firm when gently pressed with finger. Score in squares of desired size. When cool slice in squares. Makes about four dozen.

(This is an easy recipe to stir up quickly in the cool of the morning and take on an afternoon picnic.)

Autumn Harvesting

Commenced cutting and drying apples

September 4, 1848

We began to dry punkin

September 22, 1845

A light frost, the first this fall.

September 29, 1857

Made apple jelly and butter. Gathered tea leaves.

October 6, 1848

William husked corn the Sisters got shuks the next day William finished husking his corn. Tomas Shaw made crout, and the Sisters also gathered shuks.

November 7, 1845

It rained last evening enough to thoroughly lay the dust, which had become extremely annoying from its superabundance occasioned by much dry weather. The rain changed to snow, and finally to sleet and freezing and this morning the Earth appears in her white dress, and the mercury is down to 12 below zero. This is a sudden jolt for a beginning.

November 13, 1849

The Office hogs was killed

November 17, 1841

RHUBARB GOLD

7 C rhubarb, finely sliced   1 lb candy orange slices or
5 C granulated sugar   orange gum drops

Cut candy into small pieces. Mix all ingredients in large pan stirring constantly over low heat. Cook until mixture becomes clear and thickened. Pour into jar and store in refrigerator.

(When rhubarb is in your garden this is a delicious recipe to use, and is a tasty preserve to serve with hot biscuits. This can also be made with that frozen rhubarb mentioned in Rhubard Strawberry Cobbler.)

PEPPER RELISH

1 large cabbage, or two small   12 carrots
3 green peppers, stems and   ½ C salt
  seeds removed   3 pts granulated sugar
3 red sweet peppers, stems   3 pts cider vinegar
  and seeds removed   1 tsp celery seed
12 onions

Grind vegetables. Add salt. Let sit one hour or more. Squeeze juice out of vegetables with colander or food mill and add sugar, vinegar, and celery seed. Stir well and put in jars. Keeps well unsterilized but for long storage, process and seal.

SIMPLE HOMEMADE PICKLES

1 qt kosher dill pickles   1 tsp pickling spices
3 C granulated sugar   ½ C cider vinegar

Pour liquid off pickles. If not sliced, slice to desired thickness. Save the jar for later storage. Place pickles in large enough bowl to stir. Place sugar and spices on top of pickles. Pour vinegar over all. Stir with rubber spatula until all pickles are coated. Let stand one hour or longer stirring occasionally. Sugar will completely dissolve. Return to jar and store in refrigerator until ready to serve.

(This recipe adds a homemade taste to bought pickles. If your cucumber crop fails, you will still have delicious pickles, and if your homemade pickle recipe disappoints you; reprocess in this way.)

GREEN TOMATO RELISH

1 peck green tomatoes, 8 qts approximately	6 medium size onions
1 C salt	6 red sweet peppers
1 medium size head cabbage, optional	8 C granulated sugar
	3 pts cider vinegar
	2 T mixed pickling spices

Grind tomatoes. Add salt and stir. Let stand overnight then drain well. Grind cabbage, onions, and peppers. Drain. Stir into the tomatoes. Mix sugar with vinegar and stir until dissolved. Tie spice in cheese cloth bag. Pour vinegar mixture over relish and add spice bag. Simmer about 30 minutes, remove spice bag. Seal in hot sterilized jars.

END OF THE GARDEN RELISH

¼ bushel green tomatoes	2 T whole cloves
12 medium onions	2 sticks cinnamon
1 C salt	2 T ground ginger
3 qts cider vinegar	1 T celery seed
4 lbs brown sugar	4 sweet green peppers
2 T dry mustard	8 sweet red peppers

Thinly slice green tomatoes and onions. Sprinkle with salt. Let stand overnight. Drain well and wash off salt with cold water. In cheese cloth bag tie up mustard, cloves, cinnamon, ginger, and celery seed. In large pan heat vinegar and add sugar, stirring until dissolved. Put in bag of spices and cook to boiling point. Seed and remove membranes from peppers. Coarsely chop green and red peppers. Add peppers to tomato mixture and stir. Add mixture to hot vinegar. Cook slowly about one hour until tomatoes are clear. Put in hot sterilized jars and seal.

(If you do not wish to seal this relish, it will keep quite a long while in the refrigerator, or a dark cool place. If you prefer, tomatoes and onions may be chopped.)

PICKLED BEETS

1 gal sliced or diced cooked
beets
2 C cider vinegar
2 C beet juice

2 C granulated sugar
1 tsp allspice
1 tsp salt

Drain beets, saving juice. Place beets in sterilized jars. Bring other ingredients to slow simmering boil. Pour over beets. Process according to your canning instructions.

HERBED APPLE JELLY

Place the herb of your choice in the bottom of the glass and pour in the apple jelly. Some favorite choices are angelica, apple mint, basil, costmary, lavender, lemon verbena, spearmint, rose geranium, or rose petals. Quince and apple make an excellent combination—use equal parts.

Cup of Tribulation

HERB TEA

This tea can be served with fresh lemon or orange. Try it unsweetened to enjoy the true taste of herbs. If you want to sweeten, use honey or rock candy.

Combine equal parts of the following dried herbs: mint (spearmint, orangemint, or applemint), chamomile and rosemary. Use 1 teaspoon of the herb mixture to 1 cup of boiling water. Steep for 10 minutes and serve.

CUCUMBER SOUP

1 can cream of chicken soup
1 cucumber, peeled and
  seeded

8 oz sour cream
tabasco, salt and pepper to
  taste

Cut cucumber lengthwise, peel, and scoop out seeds. Whirl in blender. Combine all ingredients and chill well before serving. Serves four. Top with chopped parsley before serving.

(So often your garden will continue to yield cucumbers after you have made enough pickles for the year. This is a good recipe for finishing this crop during the hot fall days.)

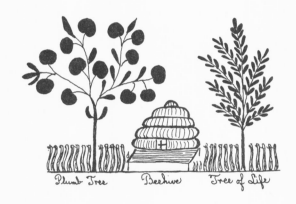

Plum Tree   Beehive   Tree of Life

OYSTER PLANT (SALSIFY) BISQUE

1 C oyster plant, sliced and
  cooked until tender, for cooking instructions see page 36
½ tsp onion, chopped

2 T celery, chopped
salt and red pepper to taste
1 to 1½ C light cream
1 egg yolk, beaten

Drain oyster plant. Blend in electric blender first three ingredients until smooth. Season. Heat in top of double boiler blended mixture and cream. Add slowly small amounts of heated bisque to egg yolk to prevent curdling. Return egg mixture to double boiler. Continue heating for about two minutes. Garnish with chopped parsley. Serve hot. Serves four.

(Salsify is an interesting vegetable whose taste is truly that of oysters. Try raising it in your garden and substitute it for that expensive seafood.)

MARINATED SALAD

1 head lettuce
1 red onion, chopped
⅓ C green pepper, chopped

½ C celery, chopped
1½ C frozen peas, 10 oz
  package, uncooked

Break half head of lettuce in small pieces. Place evenly in 13 x 9 inch glass dish. Layer onions, peppers, celery, peas, and remaining lettuce.

Mix together and spread over
  salad:
2 C mayonnaise
2 tsp lemon juice
2 T sugar

Crumble and sprinkle on
  top:
8 slices of crisp fried bacon
  strips, crumbled
8 oz cheddar cheese, grated

Cover and refrigerate overnight.

(Very fresh garden peas, uncooked are delicious in this salad.)

CUCUMBER AND NASTURTIUM SALAD

2 cucumbers
36 small nasturtium
  leaves
1 tsp Dijon mustard
2 T wine vinegar

6 T olive oil
salt, freshly ground pepper
2 T fresh tarragon, finely
  chopped
6 nasturtium flowers, optional

Peel and slice cucumbers thinly. Wash nasturtium leaves; remove stems and drain.

Combine mustard and vinegar in a bowl and stir until well blended. Add olive oil, and salt and pepper to taste, and blend well. Stir in tarragon.

When ready to serve, combine cucumbers and nasturtium leaves in a salad bowl; add vinaigrette dressing and toss well. Garnish with nasturtium flowers, if desired. Serves four to six.

31

BARBECUE SAUCE

⅔ C onions, chopped fine
6 T butter
2 C tomato catsup
⅔ C vinegar
¼ C worcestershire sauce

¼ tsp salt
¼ C brown sugar
1 C water
4 tsp prepared mustard

Sauté onions in butter, until tender. Add all other ingredients. Cook covered ten minutes. Keeps quite a while in the refrigerator.

(To cook with beef, chicken, or pork, pour desired amount of sauce over meats and bake in oven until done.)

BARBECUE ON BUN

2 lbs stew meat
½ onion, sliced

salt and pepper
1½ qt water

Combine all ingredients. Cook over low heat, stirring to prevent sticking, about four hours or until meat falls apart and almost no liquid is left. Stir in barbecue sauce. Continue cooking on low heat, stirring occasionally for two hours or until sauce boils down. Serve on warm buns. Serves about 12 to 15.

COUNTRY STEAK

2½ to 3 lbs round steak, 1¾
   inch thick
½ C all purpose flour
1 tsp salt
¼ tsp pepper
6 whole cloves
2 T or more of shortening

½ C onions, chopped
1 C celery, chopped
1 T worcestershire sauce
½ C tomato catsup
2 C beef stock, or 2 C water
   to 2 beef bouillon cubes

Beat flour into steak, first one side and then the other. Use the edge of a heavy saucer or meat pounder. Put shortening in heavy skillet and heat. Brown steak on both sides in hot fat. Put all ingredients over steak. Cover tightly and bake in oven at 350⁰ for two or more hours, until tender. Steak should be checked every hour to keep from becoming dry. Add more boiling stock or water when necessary.

DOVE BREASTS IN CREAM GRAVY

6 dove breasts
6 strips bacon
salt and pepper
1½ C heavy cream

2 tsp chopped parsley
4 T all purpose flour
3 T bacon drippings

Flour doves lightly. Fry bacon in a large iron skillet. Remove and keep warm. Sauté the dove breasts in the bacon fat, browning them well on all sides. Reduce the heat and continue cooking until they are tender, about 12 minutes. Season to taste. Remove the doves and keep warm. From skillet remove all fat but three tablespoons. Add flour and blend well. Cook until smooth and bubbly. Remove from heat and stir in cream, return to heat and cook, stirring constantly until smooth and thick. Season with salt and pepper and chopped parsley. Place dove breasts in cream gravy and garnish with bacon strips and parsley sprigs. Serve on a trivet directly from skillet.

RABBIT

Rabbit
1 C all purpose flour
salt and pepper

2 eggs
¼ C milk

Permit rabbit to soak in salt water about two hours. Pat dry. Beat eggs and milk together. Dip rabbit in egg mixture and then in flour. Repeat dipping and flouring once more. Fry in one-half inch of hot grease. Cook until golden brown and tender. Serve hot.

SCALLOPED CABBAGE

1 small head cabbage, cut into
  ½ to ¾ inch wedges
1 C cream sauce

6 slices bacon, cooked and
  crumbled

Cook cabbage quickly until barely tender. Drain well. Place in one and one-half to two quart buttered casserole dish. Pour cream sauce over casserole and top with bacon, then buttered bread crumbs. Bake at 350⁰ for 20 minutes or until lightly browned.

(This recipe can be used with left-over cooked cabbage.)

CREAM SAUCE

2 T butter
2 T all purpose flour
¼ tsp salt

⅛ tsp pepper
1 C milk

In heavy sauce pan melt butter over low heat. With wooden spoon, blend in flour and seasoning. Stir constantly until smooth and bubbly. Remove from heat. Add milk gradually and return to heat stirring all the while. Bring to a boil for one minute. Makes one cup.

BUTTERED BREAD CRUMBS

4 T butter

¾ to 1 C fresh bread crumbs,
  diced

Melt butter in sauce pan, and add crumbs. Continue stirring until lightly toasted and butter is absorbed.

(An excellent topping for most casserole dishes.)

Holy Mothers Nursery

CARROT RING

2 C carrots
1 C bread crumbs
1 C cream
3 eggs, separated

½ C celery, chopped
1 small onion, chopped
½ tsp salt
⅛ tsp pepper

Cook carrots until tender, drain and mash. Soak bread crumbs in cream, which has been combined with beaten egg yolks. Combine carrots, celery, onion, salt and pepper with cream mixture. Fold in egg whites which have been beaten stiff. Butter evenly a ring mold. Pour in carrot mixture. Bake at 325⁰ for 40 to 60 minutes or until firm. Unmold on platter, and fill center with creamed peas and mushrooms if desired.

KALE GREENS

2 lbs kale
1 ham hock, or 1 C ham scraps
(city or country)

1 qt water
salt and pepper

Wash kale carefully. Remove stalks if coarse. Boil fat in water for about 30 minutes. Strain water and return water to stove. Save larger ham pieces to add to kale later for flavor. Bring flavored water to a boil and add kale and ham scraps. Cook until desired tenderness, do not overcook as leaves should be a bit crisp. Add butter, salt and pepper to taste.

(We often have kale from the garden at Pleasant Hill in the fall after a light frost which improves the taste and texture.)

CELERY CASSEROLE

4 C celery, cut in one-inch pieces
1 can cream of chicken soup
¼ C pimientos, diced

½ C fresh bread crumbs
¼ C slivered almonds
2 T butter, melted

Boil celery in salt water about eight minutes. Drain. Add cream of chicken soup and pimientos. Put in quart greased casserole dish. Top with bread crumbs, and slivered almonds. Pour melted butter on top of casserole. Bake at 350⁰ for 35 minutes.

GREENS CASSEROLE

2 C greens, or 2 packages of   1 C cheddar cheese, grated
    frozen greens   1 egg
1 can mushroom soup   1 T onion, chopped, optional
1 C mayonnaise

Cook, drain and coarsely chop greens. Beat soup, mayonnaise, cheese, egg and onion with fork. Add greens and beat. Place in well buttered two-quart casserole dish. Top with cracker crumbs and dot with butter. Bake at 375⁰ for 30 minutes. If freezing, bake without cracker crumbs and add before rebaking. When ready to serve, heat in oven at 375⁰ until hot.

(Spinach, chard, kale, or any other type of greens, may be mixed and used in this recipe. Recipe may be placed in two one-quart casseroles, eat one and freeze one.)

SCALLOPED OYSTER PLANT (SALSIFY)

oyster plant, sliced   bread crumbs
salt   butter
paprika   cream

After digging salsify, keep two weeks in a cool place, not in refrigerator. When ready to use, slice into water to which a little flour or vinegar has been added to prevent discoloration. Drain. Add to fresh boiling water and cook until tender. Drain again. Grease baking dish. Layer crackers then oyster plant. Add seasoning and dots of butter to each layer. Pour cream about one inch deep in casserole. Top with buttered bread crumbs, see page 34. Bake at 400⁰ about 30 minutes. Serves four to six.

(Salsify can be left in ground and dug throughout winter, except for the winter of 1977.)

ONION CASSEROLE

2 lbs sliced fresh large spring onions
2 T butter
3 eggs, beaten
1 can cream of mushroom soup
¾ tsp salt
¼ tsp pepper

Cook onions a short time until just tender. Drain. Fold in remaining ingredients. Place in buttered casserole dish. Sprinkle with parmesan cheese. Top with cracker crumbs. Bake at 350° for about 30 minutes.

(If you have too many onions for your relish tray and they have gotten too big, this casserole is delicious.)

BAKED APPLES WITH RAISINS

6 medium tart apples
½ C brown sugar
1 tsp cinnamon
2 T butter
½ C raisins, seedless
½ C water

Wash and core apples. Peel a small portion from the bottom of each. Mix sugar and cinnamon. Cut butter into sugar mixture. Stir in raisins. Place apples on rack in the bottom of a heavy skillet. Fill core of apples as full as possible with sugar raisin mixture. Add water to bottom of skillet. Sprinkle remaining sugar mixture over apples. Cover skillet and bake at 350° until apples are tender. Baste often. Cooking time will vary depending on type of apples used.

(Apples are very good cooked only long enough to remain a little crisp.)

RHUBARB NUT BREAD

1½ C brown sugar
⅔ C cooking oil
1 egg
1 C buttermilk
1 tsp salt
1 tsp soda
1 tsp vanilla
2½ C flour
1½ C of diced rhubarb
½ C nuts

Mix all ingredients in order given. Fold in rhubarb and nuts. Pour into two small oiled bread pans or one large one. Bake at 325° for 40 minutes or until brown.

PUMPKIN BREAD

3½ C all purpose flour
2 tsp baking soda
1½ tsp salt
3 tsp cinnamon
3 tsp nutmeg
3 C granulated sugar

⅔ C water
1 C vegetable oil
⅔ C canned pumpkin
4 eggs
1 C nuts, optional
1 C raisins, optional

Sift flour, baking soda, salt, cinnamon, nutmeg and sugar in a bowl. Then add water, oil, pumpkin and eggs. Beat until smooth. Add nuts and raisins if desired. Pour into well greased loaf pans. Bake in 325° oven for 45 to 60 minutes. Cool ten minutes in pans. Freezes well. Makes three small loaves or one large.

(Fresh pumpkin, boiled in a small amount of water, drained and put through a sieve, can be used.)

PUMPKIN CAKE

3 C granulated sugar
1 C shortening
3 eggs, beaten slightly
2 C pumpkin, fresh or canned
1 tsp vanilla
3 C all purpose flour
½ tsp baking powder

¼ tsp salt
1 tsp soda
1 tsp cloves
1 tsp cinnamon
1 tsp nutmeg
1 tsp allspice

Cream shortening and sugar. Add beaten eggs, pumpkin and vanilla. Sift dry ingredients together and add to creamed mixture. Pre-heat over to 350°. Bake cake in a ten inch tube pan for one hour and 15 minutes, or until broom straw comes out clean when inserted into cake. Serve plain or top with whipped cream.

RHUBARB ANGELICA PIE

¼ C angelica stalk, cut in   6 T flour
  small pieces   ¼ tsp salt
4 C rhubarb, cut in ½ inch   2 T butter
  pieces   2 pie crusts, unbaked
1½ C honey

Mix first five ingredients. Pour into nine-inch pan lined with pie crust. Dot with butter. Seal top crust. Bake at 350⁰ for 45 - 55 minutes.

STACK PIES

An early Kentucky recipe which evolved because cooks did not want to carry individual pies to reunions or camp meetings.

10 egg yolks   1½ C melted butter
3 C granulated sugar   4 to 5 unbaked pie shells
1 C cream (canned milk or
  heavy cream)

Beat egg yolks until light, cream in sugar, add cream, then beat in melted butter. Leave bottom shell regular size. Make the crust in the other layers just to rim of pie pan or cut off rim. Pour mixture into shells and bake at 350⁰ or until set. If using five shells, filling will be thinner on each layer. Allow pies to cool. Take all but bottom pie from pans and stack one on top of the other, cover with caramel icing.

Icing for:

½ C butter   ¼ C milk or evaporated milk
1 C brown sugar   2 C powdered sugar

Melt butter in saucepan, add sugar. Cook five minutes, stirring constantly. Cool slightly, add milk and beat until smooth. Add powdered sugar. Cover top and sides of pies.

(A very, very rich dessert. Cut quite thin, will serve about 24.)

GREEN TOMATO MINCEMEAT

3 lbs small green tomatoes	4 lbs dark brown sugar
3 lbs tart green apples	1 T cinnamon
2 lbs seedless grapes	2 T salt
1 C cider vinegar	1 T ground nutmeg
2 T ground cloves	1 grated orange, optional

Wash, core and chop unpeeled green tomatoes. Drain the chopped tomatoes well in a colander set over a large mixing bowl. Measure the tomato juice after draining and discard. Place the tomatoes in a large enamel or stainless steel kettle, add to them the measurement of water equal to the amount of tomato juice discarded. Bring mixture to a boil, drain again through a colander, and again measure the juice and discard. Return to kettle, and add water equal to amount of water discarded, and bring to a boil. Repeat draining, measurement of discarded water, addition of water, and boiling for a third time. Wash, peel, core and chop green apples. Drain tomatoes once again, return to kettle and add all remaining ingredients, including the grated orange if desired. Bring to a boil slowly. Heat, stirring to keep mixture from sticking, for about ten minutes or until mixture is clear and marmalade-like in appearance. Ladle boiling hot mincemeat into hot sterilized preserving jars, leaving one inch from the top. Screw lids down tightly, then process jars according to instructions of your type of canner. We find it unnecessary to process jars if we use mincemeat in a month or so. For pie, mix one tablespoon of butter to one quart of mincemeat before adding to an unbaked pie crust. Also a chopped fresh apple may be added.

(This mincemeat is a good recipe for all the late tomatoes that you hate to see the first frost of the fall destroy.)

GRAPE PIE

3 eggs
1 C granulated sugar
1 C Concord grapes, seeded
dash of salt

2 T thick cream
2 T all purpose flour
1 T butter

Mix all ingredients. Pour into an unbaked crust. Bake at 375⁰ for five minutes, then reduce to 350⁰ until done. Cover with meringue and bake in a slow oven.

(There are so few things you can do with Concord grapes that this recipe will be useful.)

A Holy Plant! And fruits of Faith

MOLASSES SUGAR COOKIES

¾ C shortening
1 C granulated sugar
¼ C molasses
1 egg
2 C sifted all purpose flour

2 tsp soda
½ tsp cloves
½ tsp ginger
1 tsp cinnamon
½ tsp salt

Melt shortening in sauce pan. Remove from heat and cool. Add sugar, molasses and egg. Beat well. Sift together flour, soda, cloves, ginger, cinnamon and salt. Add molasses mixture to flour mixture. Mix well. Chill for one hour. Form in one-inch balls and roll in granulated sugar. Place on greased baking sheet. Bake at 375⁰ for eight to ten minutes. Let stand on baking sheet until cool. Remove and store in tins.

Winter Cooking

The Earth covered with sleet, the trees groaning under the weight of ice, shining as brilliant as silver blossoms. The mist and sleeting continued all day.

December 4, 1859

Divided the sugar.

January 3, 1850

A mild damp morning; but a brisk S.W. wind sprang up and played its winter life so bold and shrill, that old mercury ingloriously fled and backed down into his obscure retreat to about 14 degrees.

January 7, 1859

Mercury at 17° below in the morning, and never rose higher than one degree below zero during the day.

January 9, 1856

Killed 5 winter beeves

January 23, 1848

Saturday the brethren began to get ice

February 13, 1841

The brethren killed the last beeves.

February 16, 1841

CHEDDAR CHEESE BALL

½ lb cheddar cheese, sharp
½ C almonds, unblanched
¼ C stuffed olives, chopped
1 T pimientos, minced

2 - 3 oz packages of cream
  cheese, room temperature
½ tsp worcestershire sauce
dash of tabasco

Put cheddar cheese, almonds and olives through a food grinder. Mix in pimiento and cream cheese. Season to taste with worcestershire sauce and tabasco. Shape in ball. Roll in chopped parsley, toasted sesame seeds, chopped pecans or decorate with sliced olives. Chill until ready to serve.

(A slight bit of garlic salt may be added when mixing. Freezes well.)

SAUSAGE BALLS

3 C biscuit mix, or your favorite
  homemade biscuit recipe with
  no liquid added

1 lb of sausage
8 to 10 oz sharp cheese,
  grated

Have cheese and sausage at room temperature. Mix all ingredients together with hands. Shape into small balls. Bake at 450⁰ for ten to twelve minutes. Makes 72 sausage balls.

(Balls may be frozen uncooked. Thaw for a half hour before baking.)

INSTANT SPICED TEA

1¾ C instant dry orange
  breakfast drink
1¾ C instant tea

2¼ C granulated sugar
1½ tsp cinnamon
1½ tsp cloves

Measure ingredients in large container or jar. Stir until blended. Store in jar until needed. Shake jar before spooning out. Use two teaspoons or more of tea mixture to each teacup of boiling water when serving.

SIMPLE HOLIDAY PUNCH

1 large can red punch drink
1 large can pineapple juice
1 large can orange juice
½ small can frozen lemonade,
   or ½ C fresh lemon juice

1 qt pineapple sherbet
1 large bottle ginger ale

Mix red punch drink, pineapple, orange and lemon juice. Let stand in refrigerator until ready to serve. Standing permits juices to blend. Place sherbet in punch bowl when ready to serve. Add juice mixture. Chop sherbet a little. Pour ginger ale in slowly. Punch is ready to serve. Serves 20.

(This is a very easy punch to prepare. Juices do not have to be blended ahead if large enough container is not available, but do mix juices together before adding sherbet or ginger ale.)

Flask of Wine

CHRISTMAS PUNCH

1 gal apple cider
1 qt orange juice
1 C lemon juice
1 large can pineapple juice

24 whole cloves
1 C granulated sugar
4 sticks cinnamon

Combine all ingredients in large pan. Simmer ten minutes. Remove cinnamon and cloves. Serve hot. Makes a gallon and a half.

(This stores beautifully in the refrigerator when cool. Shake and heat desired amount to be served when guests arrive. This is also excellent when you have a cold or the flu.)

WASSAIL BOWL

1½ gal apple cider
¼ tsp salt
¾ lb dark brown sugar
1½ T whole cloves
1½ T allspice
3 sticks cinnamon

½ tsp powdered ginger
½ tsp grated nutmeg
3 lemons or limes, sliced
4½ oranges, sliced
1½ pt sherry

Mix the cider with salt and sugar. Tie spices in cloth bag and drop into cider. Bring to a hard boil, simmer fifteen minutes in a covered pot. Remove from heat and taste for desired sweetness. Add granulated sugar, a spoonful at a time, if you wish. Set aside. When ready to serve, heat to boiling and remove spice bag. Add sherry. Top with lemons and oranges. Whole baked apples studded with cloves are also a traditional garnish. Serve hot.

(The "wassail" began as an Old English drinking toast–"health to you!" We use the term for any festive punch, but in medieval custom it was associated with the Christmas Holidays; a hot mixture of spice, fruit and beer was passed around the table to toast the season and the company. "Wassail bowls" in later English custom were decorated with ribbons and sprigs of rosemary and carried about by singers. "Wassail songs" recall the occasions when revelers toasted the holidays and children went from door to door caroling and begging treats.)

BUN STICKS

Split hot dog buns and cut each into four lengthwise pieces. Brush each side with melted butter. Put on a cookie sheet in 350⁰ oven. Let sticks dry out and get lightly brown and crisp. Serve hot.

(For variety sprinkle with poppy seed, garlic salt or any other herb seasoning. Delicious served with soup.)

CRABMEAT SOUP

1 can cream of celery soup
1 can cream of asparagus soup
½ C cream

1½ soup cans of milk
1 can king crabmeat, tendons removed

Fix in top of double boiler. Mix the soups well. Gradually add cream and milk, stirring until smooth. At the last minute before serving add drained crabmeat. Stir lightly so that crabmeat does not crumble.

(Lobster may be substituted, if desired, for crabmeat. A little sherry may be added for flavor.)

※ ※ ※ ※ ※

AVOCADO SALAD MOLD

1 package lemon flavored
gelatin, 6 oz
1 C boiling water
3 T lemon juice
½ tsp salt

½ C mayonnaise
1 C avocado, peeled and mashed
½ pt heavy cream, whipped

Dissolve gelatin in water. Add lemon juice and salt. Cool in refrigerator. When slightly jelled, whip with electric mixer. Stir mayonnaise into avocado and then fold in cream. Stir mixture slowly into gelatin mixture. Rinse ring mold in cold water. Shake off excess water. Put salad in mold and place in refrigerator until set. Unmold and serve on lettuce leaves.

(This salad can be served with citrus fruit).

48

MOLDED SEAFOOD SALAD

1 large box lemon gelatin (6 oz)
¾ C boiling water
¾ C cold water
3 T lemon juice

1 bottle tomato chili sauce,
  12 oz
3 T horseradish
2 - 4½ oz cans shrimp

Dissolve gelatin in boiling water. Stir in cold water. Mix all remaining ingredients, except shrimp, and add to gelatin. Fold in shrimp and pour in mold that has been rinsed in cold water. Refrigerate until set. Unmold and serve on lettuce leaves. Serves about 12.

※ ※ ※ ※ ※

HOT BROWN

4 slices of bread, toasted
4 nice size slices of turkey
  or chicken
8 slices of bacon, slightly
  cooked, or 4 slices thinly-
  sliced country ham

½ C American cheese,
  grated
½ C sharp cheese,
  grated

Cream sauce as follows:

2 T butter
2 T flour
1 C milk

salt and cayenne to taste
¼ tsp curry powder if
  desired

    ¼ C American and ¼ C sharp cheese, grated and mixed

Melt butter. Add flour, salt, cayenne and curry if desired. Stir constantly until smooth and bubbly. Remove from heat and add milk, stirring all the while until smooth. Return to heat and cook slowly until thickened. Stir in cheeses until melted.

To assemble place turkey or chicken on toast in four ovenware dishes and cover with cream sauce. Top with grated cheeses then bacon or ham. Place under broiler (about six inches) and broil slowly until bacon is cooked. Serve hot from broiler. Serves four.

(A true Kentucky recipe since it was created at the wonderful old Brown Hotel in Louisville. This is one of many variations and it is a good way to use up that Thanksgiving turkey).

BOTTOM ROUND OF BEEF

1 bottom round of beef   2 T salt
3 T worcestershire sauce

Place beef on rack in roasting pan. Sprinkle worcestershire sauce and salt over the meat. Fill roaster with water until half way up on beef. Roast at 350⁰ for three to four hours or until done, depending on size. You may need to add hot water during cooking time. Do not let roast get dry.

HORSERADISH SAUCE

½ C mayonnaise   ⅓ C prepared horseradish,
½ C heavy cream, whipped   drained
tabasco to taste   worcestershire sauce
⅛ tsp dry mustard

Combine mayonnaise and whipped cream. Season highly with tabasco and a few drops of worcestershire sauce. Stir in dry mustard and horseradish.

(This sauce is very good with cold sliced roast beef or turkey.)

BAKED HAM SLICES WITH SCALLOPED POTATOES

1 inch ham slice, or 1 qt ham   ½ medium onion, chopped
  chunks   2 T all purpose flour
7 medium potatoes, sliced   2 T butter
salt and pepper   hot milk

In greased baking dish arrange one thin layer of raw potatoes. Sprinkle layer with salt, pepper, onions, flour and pieces of butter. Place ham slices on layer. Fill around and over ham with remaining potatoes and seasoning. If using ham chunks, add with each layer. Pour hot milk over potatoes and ham one-half to three-quarter inch from top of potatoes. Bake 350⁰ uncovered about one and one-half hours or until potatoes are done.

(This is a good way to use up the end of your ham.)

BEEF HASH

2 C beef broth or 2 boullion
   cubes to 2 C boiling water
4 C beef, cooked and cubed
4 T butter
4 T flour

¼ tsp worcestershire sauce
¼ C onions, chopped
salt and pepper to taste
dash of red pepper

Heat butter and add flour, stirring constantly. Add broth slowly, stirring until thickened. Add worcestershire sauce and onions. Cool for a little while and add salt and pepper to taste. Add beef, and serve hot. Serves six to eight. May need to be thinned with hot stock if set out a while.

(Delicious with Indian griddle cakes, see **We Make You Kindly Welcome,** *page 4.)*

FRIED CORN MEAL MUSH

3 C water
a little salt

1 C corn meal
1 C cold water

Bring three cups of water to a boil and add salt. Add meal to cold water and gradually add to boiling water. Stir well while cooking. When done (will be very thick and bubbly) mold in can or pan and allow to stand overnight. Slice and roll in meal. Pan fry when ready to serve.

(Many people think of fried mush as served only with syrup. A tradition in our family was to serve it with roasts and gravy. Also excellent topped with hash.)

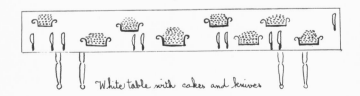
White table with cakes and knives

OVEN-GLAZED CHICKEN

8 chicken breasts
4 T shortening
salt, pepper and flour to season
   chicken
3 T butter

¼ C almonds, slivered
¼ C lemon juice
1 C water
1 C sherry

Set oven at 325°. Lightly dust chicken breasts with flour, On top of stove, brown skin side down in skillet or heavy pan in shortening. Turn. Season. In another pan mix sherry, lemon juice, water and butter; cook until butter melts. Add half of this mixture to chicken breasts. When sauce begins to boil, cover pan tightly and bake in oven one hour. Uncover and add rest of mixture and almonds. Recover and cook one-half hour longer. Check almonds, if they are not brown, uncover and cook until they are nicely toasted.

Plate of Cakes

SAUSAGE AND EGG CASSEROLE

8 eggs, hard boiled and
   sliced

8 sausage patties or links,
   cooked

3 C cream sauce

Cream sauce as follows:

6 T butter
6 T all purpose flour
¾ tsp salt

½ tsp pepper
3 C milk

In pan melt butter. Stir in flour, salt and pepper with wooden spoon. Cook over low heat, stirring until mixture is smooth and bubbly. Remove from heat. Stir in milk. Return to heat, stirring constantly, and bring to a boil. Boil one minute.

Mix lightly sausage, eggs and cream sauce in buttered casserole dish. Top with cracker crumbs. Bake at 375° for 20 minutes. Serves six to eight.

NOODLE RING

1 C noodles	1 T celery, chopped
1½ C milk	1 T onions, chopped
1 small package Velveeta cheese	1 T parsley, chopped
3 T butter	1 T pimientoes, chopped
3 eggs	½ tsp salt
1 C soft bread crumbs	¼ tsp red pepper

Cook noodles and drain. Heat milk and melt cheese and butter in milk. Beat eggs and add to milk along with noodles, bread crumbs and other ingredients. Bake in well-greased ring mold or casserole at 350° for about 35 minutes.

PARSNIPS

2 C diced parsnips	2 T parsley, chopped
1 to 2 T butter, to taste	dash of cinnamon

Dice parsnips, core if large. Drop into water, enough to cover, to which a small amount of flour has been added to prevent discoloration. Drain. Put parsnips in boiling water, to which a dash of cinnamon has been added, and cook until tender, about ten minutes, depending on age and size of parsnips. Drain. Chop parsley into melted butter, add to parsnips and toss well. Season with salt, pepper and a dash of cinnamon.

(From my childhood on I disliked parsnips in any form, a prejudice I passed on to one of my daughters. My other daughter and her husband, however, strongly recommend this recipe. They are particularly fond of parsnips dug after winter has begun. Parsnips planted in the spring may be harvested through the early spring of the following year; indeed, my son-in-law assures me, a parsnip dug after the first spring thaw is particularly good.

Large parsnips should be cored; the woody center is the source of the tough, strong taste which many people dislike.)

BAKED TANGERINES IN SHELLS

6 tangerines	¾ C orange juice
2 T brown sugar	2 T butter

Peel tangerines down about one third from top. Fill each center with one tsp of the sugar and dot with butter. Pour orange juice over each tangerine. Bake at 325° for 30 minutes. Makes six servings.

BANANA SCALLOPS

6 bananas, peeled
1 egg, slightly beaten

½ C finely crushed corn flakes
1½ tsp salt

Cut bananas in one-inch slices and dip them in mixture of egg and salt. Drain, then roll in corn flakes. Fry in hot deep fat, 375⁰, for one to two minutes or until brown. Drain on paper towel. Serve very hot. Serves six.

(Excellent as a vegetable substitute.)

* * * * *

HOLIDAY SWEET BREAD

2 pkgs dry yeast
5¼ to 5½ C all purpose
    flour, sifted
1 C milk
½ C butter

1 C granulated sugar
¼ tsp salt
3 eggs, slightly beaten
½ C mashed potatoes,
    unseasoned

Combine yeast and two cups of flour in large bowl. Heat together, until just warm, milk, butter, sugar and salt; stirring occasionally. Add to dry mixture. Stir in eggs and potatoes. Beat with electric mixer at low speed for half a minute. Beat for three minutes at high speed. By hand, stir in enough of remaining flour to make a moderately stiff dough. Turn out on a floured surface. Knead eight to ten minutes until smooth and elastic. Place in greased bowl; turning once to grease all of surface. Cover and let rise until double in bulk, about 1½ hours. Punch down. Divide dough into two parts. Cover and let rest ten minutes. This bread may be baked in a nine-inch round cake pan or four small loaf pans. When ready to bake, grease pans. Shape dough into eight 2½ inch balls and place around edges of cake pan or shape into 16 balls and fill four small loaf pans. Let rise until light, 45 minutes to one hour. Bake at 375⁰ for 20 to 25 minutes. Remove from pans and cool on rack.

(This is an excellent bread "as is", but raisins, nuts or candied fruits can be added as well as a simple glaze.)

SALT RISING BREAD

Start early before you plan to make bread. Have one empty 3 lb shortening or coffee can for convenience in mixing starter.

1 C milk, scalded	⅛ tsp soda
7 T white corn meal	½ tsp granulated sugar
¼ tsp salt	

After scalding milk, remove film and pour back and forth between can and pan to cool slightly. Pour milk into can and add the above ingredients. Cover and keep in a warm place until next morning. This batter will become light, puffy and full of bubbles.

Next morning:

1 C warm water	⅛ tsp soda
½ tsp salt	2½ C flour

Add second ingredients to can and mix well. Batter will be stiff. Allow to rise to top of can in a warm spot.

In a bowl have ready:

6 C flour	1 T granulated sugar
1 tsp salt	½ C shortening

Cut shortening into flour, salt and sugar in large mixing bowl. When starter mixture in can has risen to top, pour into mixture in bowl. Add ¾ C warm water and stir in well. Batter will become very stiff. Work dough with hands until smooth. When dough is ready, shape into three loaves. Place in ungreased loaf pans 3 x 7. Brush top of loaves with soft butter. Allow to rise again in a warm place. Bake at 325° for five to ten minutes then at 350° for about 45 minutes.

(From my childhood on, I have always loved to use this bread for breakfast toast. There are many wonderful cooks in my hometown of Cynthiana, all of whom have a recipe for salt rising bread.)

STEAMED CHRISTMAS BREAD

2 eggs
2 bananas, cut in small pieces
1 peeled apple, chopped
1 tsp baking soda
1 tsp cinnamon
½ tsp salt
½ tsp nutmeg

¼ tsp ginger
1 tsp vanilla
¼ C shortening
1¼ C granulated sugar
1½ C all purpose flour
1½ C light raisins

In electric blender combine first nine ingredients. In bowl, cut shortening into sugar and stir in the blended mixture. Coat raisins with flour and add. Pour batter into cans and cover with foil. Place in a large kettle with enough hot water to come half way up on the side of cans. Cover kettle and steam in 325° oven for two hours. When finished cooking, open closed end of can and push out. Freezes well.

(Have on hand three empty #303 cans, equivalent to two cups. Dough will be steamed in these and is easily removed.)

OATMEAL BREAD

1½ C quick rolled oats,
   uncooked
⅓ C granulated sugar
2 T salt

4 C boiling water
1 T dry yeast
8¾ C all purpose flour

Mix oatmeal, sugar, salt and water. Let sit until lukewarm. Stir in yeast. Add flour and stir well. Cover and let rise. When double in bulk, punch down and let rise again until double. Punch down again and divide into three loaves. Let rise to double bulk in slightly-greased bread pans. Bake at 400° for 20 minutes, then turn oven down to 325° for another 20 minutes. Let cool slightly and remove from pans.

(This is a dry bread and very good for breakfast toast.)

OATMEAL PIE

¾ C granulated sugar　　　¾ C quick rolled oats,
6 T butter　　　　　　　　　uncooked
¾ C corn syrup　　　　　　2 eggs
　　　　　　　　　　　　　1 tsp vanilla

Mix together granulated sugar, corn syrup and butter. Fold in slightly beaten eggs. Add vanilla and stir in oats. Pour in unbaked pie shell. Bake at 350⁰ for 30 to 35 minutes.

❊　❊　❊　❊　❊

PRUNE WHIP

1 C well-cooked pitted prunes　　2 scant T granulated sugar
a few grains of salt　　　　　　　1 egg white

Put cooked prunes through sieve. Add salt, egg white and sugar. Whip with electric mixer until it holds a peak. Chill. Serve in mound on custard. Makes about eight servings.

(This recipe can be varied with other dried or well-drained fruit, such as apricots.)

CUSTARD FOR PRUNE WHIP

2 C milk　　　　　　　　　½ C granulated sugar
1 T all purpose flour　　　　1 tsp vanilla, optional
3 egg yolks

Reserve one-half cup of the milk and mix with flour. Set aside. In top of double boiler place remaining milk. Put over lightly boiling water and scald. Skim off film if it forms. Add flour-milk mixture. Stir with fork. Lightly beat egg yolks and sugar. Add small amount of milk to egg mixture slowly to prevent curdling. Add the rest of milk slowly and return to double boiler. Cook until thickened or will coat a spoon. Flavor with vanilla. Chill. When ready to serve pour custard in individual dessert dishes. Place mound of prune whip on custard. Serve immediately.

LEMON TARTS

2 eggs, slightly beaten   1 T lemon juice
1 C granulated sugar   1 T grated lemon rind
¼ tsp salt   2 T butter, melted

Combine eggs, sugar and salt. Beat slightly to blend. Stir in remaining ingredients. Pour into unbaked tart cups, not fluted. Bake at 375⁰ for 14 to 20 minutes until crust is brown and filling puffed. Makes about 14.

(If tart shells are not available, make tart shells in muffin tins.)

FUDGE CAKE

1 C water   ½ tsp salt
4 T cocoa   1 tsp soda
1 C butter   ½ C buttermilk
2 C all purpose flour   2 eggs, well beaten
2 C granulated sugar

Let water, cocoa, and butter come to a boil, mixing well. Cool. Add cocoa mixture to the remaining ingredients. Mix well. Bake 20 minutes at 350⁰ in a greased sheet cake pan 17 x 11 x ¾. Before cake is done, begin mixing icing.

FUDGE CAKE ICING

4 T cocoa   6 T milk
4 T butter   1 lb box powdered sugar

Heat and blend cocoa, butter and milk. With electric mixer beat in powdered sugar until smooth. Spread over hot cake immediately after removing from oven. Let cool completely. Serve directly from pan.

(This is a good cool weather cake, but on warm days icing becomes very sticky. This icing is also an excellent glaze for doughnuts.)

RUM CAKE

3 sticks butter
1 - 8 oz package cream cheese
3 C granulated sugar
1½ tsp rum flavoring

dash of salt
6 large eggs, beaten
3 C cake flour
almost 1 pt light rum

Cream butter, cream cheese and sugar together. Stir in salt and rum flavoring. Add eggs, one at a time, and blend. Add flour gradually, mixing thoroughly. Pour in ten-inch well-greased tube cake pan. Bake at 325⁰ for one hour and fifteen minutes or more. Let cool in pan for five minutes. Remove from pan and prick all over with fork. Pour rum very slowly over cake so all will be absorbed. Before serving sprinkle with powdered sugar.

Branch of Purity

ORANGE CAKE

1 C butter
1¾ C granulated sugar
4 eggs
1 tsp soda
½ tsp salt
3½ C all purpose flour, sifted

½ C buttermilk
2 C dates, chopped
1 lb candy orange slices,
  finely cut
1 C coconut, shredded
1 C pecans, chopped

Cream butter and sugar thoroughly. Add eggs one at a time and beat. Mix soda and salt with flour and add alternately with buttermilk to butter mixture, beginning and ending with flour. Add remaining ingredients mixing well. Pour into greased and floured or lined tube pan. Bake at 270⁰ to 300⁰ for two and one-half hours or until done. While cake is still hot and in pan, mix topping:

1 C fresh orange juice
2 C powdered sugar

Pour over hot cake. Remove cake from pan when topping has been absorbed. Do not serve immediately, allow to stand and mellow several hours or overnight.

PLEASANT HILL CHRISTMAS CAKE

¾ C butter
1½ C granulated sugar
1 C milk
1 tsp vanilla
3 C all purpose flour, sifted
3 tsp baking powder

¼ tsp salt
3 egg whites, beaten
   until stiff
½ C black walnuts, hickory
   nuts or pecans, chopped

Sift flour, baking powder and salt together. Cream butter and sugar until very light. Add alternately flour and milk. Stir in vanilla. Fold in egg whites and then nuts. Pour into two greased and lightly floured eight-inch cake pans. Bake at 350° for about 30 minutes. Frost with *Maple Syrup Frosting.*

MAPLE SYRUP FROSTING

1 C maple syrup
2 egg whites, unbeaten
¼ tsp salt

½ C black walnuts, hickory
   nuts or pecans, chopped

Cook maple syrup to 242° - 248° on candy thermometer or until a firm ball forms when dropped into cold water. Pour syrup slowly into egg whites beating all the time. Add salt and beat until thick. Frost cake and sprinkle nuts on top of frosting.

(This icing does not set hard.)

POUND CAKE

½ C shortening
1 C butter
3 C granulated sugar
5 eggs, separated

3 C all purpose flour
1 tsp baking powder
1 C sweet milk
2 tsp vanilla

With electric mixer cream butter, shortening and sugar until fluffy. Add egg yolks one at a time. Sift flour with baking powder and add alternately with milk to batter. Add vanilla. Beat egg whites stiff and fold into batter. Bake in bundt or angel food cake pan at 325° for one and one-half hours. Time may vary according to your oven.

BASIC FROSTING

⅓ C shortening
3 C powdered sugar

5 T sweet milk
1 tsp vanilla

Mix sugar with shortening. Beat in milk one tablespoon at a time until at a desired spreading consistency. Add vanilla and continue beating at high speed until smooth and creamy, approximately three to five minutes. Recipe will cover a sheet cake or one layer cake.

(If you want to use this frosting for decorating a cake, use less milk and shortening as decorative frosting must be stiff. Vegetable shortening is used because it gives a very white icing.)

❊ ❊ ❊ ❊ ❊

RAISIN COOKIES

½ C raisins
1 T granulated sugar used to
  cook raisins
¾ C granulated sugar
1 egg

1 tsp vanilla
1½ C all purpose flour
1 tsp baking powder
¼ tsp salt
½ C butter

Boil raisins and sugar in enough water to cover until soft (about ten minutes) drain well. Set aside. Cream butter and sugar until well blended. Beat in egg and vanilla, mixing well. Sift dry ingredients together. Add this to creamed mixture. Chill for at least two hours then roll on floured surface. Roll out dough to one-fourth inch thick. With a three inch diameter circular cookie cutter, cut out cookies. You will need two cut-outs for each cookie. Drop small amount of drained raisins, about one teaspoonful, in center of one cookie layer. Place other layer on top. Press gently around edges to seal. Sprinkle with granulated or colored sugar. Place on greased cookie sheet. Bake at 400⁰ until edges are slightly browned. Store in tins. Makes 12 large cookies.

(Men and children seem to love large cookies, but for a smaller cookie place raisins on one cut circle of dough and then fold over and seal and sprinkle with sugar. These cookies may also be filled with small amounts of mincemeat or green tomato mincemeat.)

ORANGE MARMALADE COOKIES

2 C all purpose flour, sifted
½ tsp baking powder
½ tsp salt
2 C quick rolled oats (uncooked)
1⅓ C butter

1 C granulated sugar
2 eggs
1 tsp vanilla
¼ C orange marmalade
1 tsp orange rind

Sift together flour, baking powder, salt; stir oats into flour. Cream butter and sugar until smooth. Add eggs and vanilla; beat until light and fluffy. Stir in dry ingredients, marmalade and rind. Drop by teaspoonsful onto well-greased baking sheet. Bake at 350° for 12 to 15 minutes, or until lightly browned around the edges. Remove cookies from oven when done and place on wire rack to cool. Ice with orange glaze. (See below.)

ORANGE GLAZE

2 C sifted powdered sugar   3 T fresh orange juice

Beat together sugar and juice. Ice cookies, let dry before storing.

❋ ❋ ❋ ❋ ❋

CRUNCHY COOKIES

1 C granulated sugar
1 C corn syrup

1 C peanut butter
6 C Rice Krispies

Bring sugar and corn syrup to a boil. Take off stove and add peanut butter and stir well. Stir this mixture into cereal. Place in greased 9 x 11 pan and press down.

Topping for:

1 - 6 oz package of
chocolate morsels

1 - 6 oz package of
butterscotch morsels

Melt these together over boiling water and spread on top of cereal mixture. Cut in squares.

CARAMEL PRESS COOKIES

1 C soft butter
¾ C light brown sugar, firmly
 packed
1 egg yolk

¼ tsp salt
½ tsp vanilla
2 C all purpose flour

Cream butter and brown sugar until light and fluffy. Add egg yolks, vanilla and salt. Blend in flour. Place dough in cookie press. Press cookies onto greased baking sheet. Sprinkle tops of cookies with granulated sugar or colored sugar. Bake at 350⁰ about eight minutes or until lightly browned. Cool on wire rack. Makes about seven dozen cookies.

(This is a very quick cookie recipe with a delicious brown sugar taste.)

KENTUCKY BOURBON BALLS

3½ to 4 C powdered sugar
½ C butter
4 T, or less, bourbon

4 squares semi-sweet
 chocolate
¼ bar parafin

Cream butter. Add sugar gradually. Beat well. Slowly add bourbon, blending well. Chill, about one hour or more. Roll in one inch balls and place on waxed paper. Lightly press a pecan on top. Chill for one hour or more. In top of double boiler melt chocolate and parafin and stir to blend. Dip with fork and return to waxed paper. Chill. Store in tins in refrigerator.

(I use my old-fashioned wooden handle, three-prong fork for dipping. Strength of bourbon flavoring depends on proof and taste. If creamed mixture seems too sticky, beat in a little more powdered sugar.)

Food for All Seasons

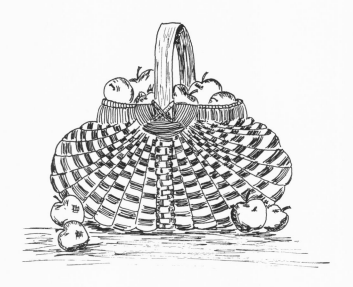

Mercury at 37, snow thawing considerably. It sprinkled rain most of the day, and about dusk it terminated in a violent snow storm for a few minutes; and the face of the Earth, which had began to peep out in spots, suddenly retreated and resumed her white veil, to the great annoyance of her inhabitants

February 16, 1856

The brethren replanted the sage.

April 15, 1850

All hands turned out and gathered strawberries and made 95 lbs of preserves.

May 26, 1849

Gleaned the cherrey trees and made preserves

June 19, 1849

Malinda took honey and stored it away

July 17, 1849

The drougth continues to a distressing extent. The pastures are dried up, the corn is cut short

August 19, 1860

The brethren began to get out wheat.

August 30, 1841

SLUMBER PARTY BREAKFAST

Fry bacon crisp. Toast insides of hot dog buns. Fill with strips of bacon and replace tops. Serve with a pitcher of orange juice and hot chocolate or milk.

(Have plenty on hand.)

BREAKFAST SOUFFLE

1½ lb pork sausage
9 eggs, beaten slightly
3 C milk
1½ tsp dry mustard

1 tsp salt
3 slices bread, cut in ⅛ inch
  cubes
1½ C cheddar cheese, grated

Brown sausage and drain. Spread in a 9 x 13 x 2 inch greased pan. Mix all other ingredients and spread over sausage; cover pan and refrigerate overnight. Bake uncovered for one hour at 350⁰.

BREAKFAST BACON COOKIES

1 C all purpose flour, unsifted
¾ C granulated sugar
¼ tsp baking soda
½ C cooked strips of bacon,
  crumbled

½ C butter
1 egg, beaten
2 C raisin bran flakes
  cereal

Mix in bowl flour, sugar, and soda. Add bacon bits, butter and egg. Mix well and stir in cereal. Drop by teaspoonsful on an ungreased cookie sheet two inches apart. Bake at 350⁰ until brown. Cool slightly before removing from pan. Makes two dozen.

PARTY BREAKFAST BANANAS

Leaving skin on, split a whole banana lengthwise and pierce with fork from end to end. Squeeze wedge of lemon over banana and sprinkle with granulated sugar. Serve immediately.

(A good breakfast dish or something different for dessert. For each person, serve one banana on a plate with a lemon wedge and let your family prepare their own.)

ONION ROUNDS

Cover small round of white bread or toast with thin slices of onions. Spread with mayonnaise, sprinkle with parmesan or very sharp grated cheese and broil until brown.

CHEESE STRAWS

2 C all purpose flour
1¾ C sharp cheese, grated
⅔ C butter

dash of red pepper
3 T cold water

Cut butter into flour with pastry cutter. Stir in cheese and pepper. Sprinkle with water. Stir with fork and work into dough. Roll out on floured board. Cut in narrow strips with fluted pastry wheel, about three inches long. Bake at 350° for about ten minutes. Makes about 150.

(Extra good sprinkled with a little grated parmesan cheese before baking.)

SHRIMP NEWBURG

8 oz shrimp
4 T butter
1 T all purpose flour
½ tsp salt
¼ tsp red pepper

dash nutmeg
1 C cream or half and half
1 egg yolk
2 T sherry

Melt butter in a sauce pan; stir in flour, salt, pepper and nutmeg. Cook, stirring constantly, until bubbly. Stir in cream; continue cooking and stirring until sauce thickens and boils one minute. Beat egg yolks in a bowl; beat in slowly about half of hot sauce to prevent curdling, then stir back into remaining sauce in pan. Cook, stirring constantly, one minute. Stir in sherry. Add shrimp when ready to serve.

(Keep shrimp newberg warm in chafing dish. Serve in tiny tart shells.)

SHRIMP AND SAUCES

Serve whole shrimp on bowl of ice. Garnish with lemon wedges and parsley. The two following recipes are easy and good.

1 C mayonnaise	½ tsp celery salt
2 scant tsp sweet pickle, chopped	tabasco to taste
	½ tsp dry mustard
½ tsp capers, drained and chopped	½ tsp chives
	½ scant tsp chopped parsley
½ tsp anchovy paste	¼ C thin french dressing

Mix together and chill before serving.

3 T horseradish	4 drops tabasco
1 C tomato catsup	1½ tsp worcestershire sauce
1 T lemon juice	
½ tsp salt	

Mix together and chill before serving.

(It is nice to serve both of these sauces one on each side of shrimp bowl to please all tastes.)

Rabbit

MARINATED MUSHROOMS

3 T plus 1 tsp dark wine vinegar	1 T lemon juice
3 T plus 1 tsp sherry	4 drops tabasco sauce
6 T plus 2 tsp olive oil	1 small garlic clove, chopped
pinch of salt	1 lb can mushrooms or 1 lb fresh mushrooms
1 tsp sugar	

Bring first eight ingredients to boil and pour over mushrooms. Let stand in covered jar in refrigerator at least 24 hours. This will keep quite a while.

(If using fresh mushrooms add to marinade when it starts to boil, and should boil for three minutes, covered.)

HERB MUSTARD

½ lb jar commercial salad
mustard
9 T brown sugar
1 T dried lemon thyme
1 tsp dried sweet marjoram
1 tsp dried spearmint

1 tsp dried sweet or lemon
basil
1 tsp powdered coriander
¼ tsp celery salt
¾ C mayonnaise

Add sugar to mustard and mix until sugar is dissolved. Add all dried, crumbled herbs, coriander and celery salt. Blend mayonnaise in thoroughly. Keep under refrigeration. Allow about two weeks for complete blending of flavors.

HERB VINEGAR

Depending on the type of vinegar used, different herbs will yield appealing blends. With white vinegar, try chives, tarragon, mint, or salad burnet. With apple cider vinegar, try a herb blend, or mint, basil, or garlic. For wine vinegar, use a basil and garlic mix.

Crush or bruise three handfuls of fresh herbs for each half gallon of vinegar. Place the vinegar in a pot on the stove. Heat thoroughly, but do not boil. Pour hot vinegar over herbs in storage jar or bottle and cover tightly. Shake often. Store for four to six weeks. Strain into smaller bottles, discarding herbs. Cap and store till needed.

A Strawberry Vine

ICED TEA PUNCH

2 qts water
⅓ C black tea
1 qt orange juice, cold

1⅓ C granulated sugar
1 C lemon juice, cold
1 qt ginger ale, cold

Bring one quart water to a full boil. Pour over tea, cover and let brew five minutes. Strain into a gallon container. Stir in sugar until dissolved. Add the other quart of water at faucet temperature and fruit juices. Refrigerate until ready to serve. When ready to serve pour over ice cubes in a punch bowl or pitcher. Add ginger ale and garnish with orange and lemon slices. This recipe makes about 40 four-ounce cups.

(You may add rum, if desired, to suit taste.)

FRUIT PUNCH WITH ICE RING

2 qts orange juice
2 large cans pineapple
   juice

2 large cans of frozen
   lemonade
1 qt ginger ale

Blend juices and let stand until ready to serve. Pour in ginger ale just before serving and float ice ring on top.

(Frozen juice is less orange in color than canned.)

ICE RING

Place strawberries, lemon slices, or other fruit in bottom of ring round mold. Mint leaves make a nice contrasting color. Put small amount of water in ring and place in freezer until set. When frozen hard add more water to mold and freeze until ready to use. May be made several days in advance.

71

PARTY PUNCH DRY

3 large bottles of ginger ale
1-16 oz can frozen lemonade
3 qts water

1 large bottle soda water
1 package frozen straw-
berries

Thaw strawberries enough to separate and arrange in ring mold. Add small amount of water and freeze. This will prevent strawberries from floating. When firm add enough water to almost fill mold. Put in freezer. Freeze solid. This may be done days ahead of time. In separate container mix lemonade and water. Put mixture in punch bowl. Add ginger ale and soda water before serving. Float strawberry ice ring in punch.

NOODLE SALAD

1 16 oz package bowtie egg
noodles
1 small bunch celery, cut into
bite-size pieces
8 hard cooked eggs, sliced
4 medium tomatoes, cut into
wedges

1 C bottled oil and vinegar
dressing with herbs and
spices
3 tsp salt
2 tsp dill weed

Prepare noodles as package directs; drain well. In large bowl, toss noodles with remaining ingredients until well mixed. Cover and refrigerate, tossing occasionally. Makes 12 servings.

BANANA CROQUETTES

1 small or ½ large banana,
peeled

country dressing, page 8
peanuts, finely chopped

Coat banana with country dressing and roll in peanuts. Serve on lettuce.

(Your children will love it.)

GRAPEFRUIT, FIG OR DATE SALAD

Peel and section grapefruit. Serve on lettuce leaves with dates or figs stuffed with slightly thinned cream cheese. Top with small amount of your favorite salad dressing.

PARTY MOLDED SALAD

1 package lime flavored
  gelatin, 3 oz
1 package lemon flavored
  gelatin, 3 oz
1 C mayonnaise
2 C boiling water
1 small can condensed milk
  (unsweetened)
2 small cans crushed
  pineapple (drained)
1 C small curd cottage cheese
1 C chopped pecans

This party salad may be prepared and served three ways, depending on your party needs:

(1) Combine lime and lemon gelatin; mix well with mayonaise. Add boiling water and stir until gelatin is dissolved. Add condensed milk. Fold pineapple, cottage cheese and nuts together gently; place in mold and add gelatin mixture. Stir slightly to be sure salad is well blended. Chill until firm. Remove from mold and serve with crisp lettuce.

(2) For an attractive layered mold combine gelatin, mayonaise, boiling water and condensed milk as above. Pour a small amount of this mixture (one-half to one inch, depending on your mold) into chilled mold and refrigerate until firm. Meanwhile, fold pineapple and cottage cheese into remaining mixture. Spoon into mold on top of firm layer. Then press pecans into mixture, being sure nuts are covered but form a "crust." When unmolding, loosen edges with knife and dip mold briefly into warm water.

(3) For easy serving to a large number of people, you may simply add pineapple, cottage cheese and nuts to gelatin mixture. Place in long baking dish, chill, cut into squares and serve on crisp lettuce with a dab of mayonaise.

(This is a rich, sweet salad which goes well with ham and adds a lively touch to a buffet.)

BLUE CHEESE MOLDS

1 envelope unflavored gelatin
⅓ C milk
1 package (8 oz) cream cheese
at room temperature
1 package (4 oz) blue cheese,
crumbled

⅓ C salad dressing
1 T lemon juice
⅛ tsp salt

Combine cheeses and blend until smooth. Soften gelatin in milk for about five minutes. Then melt over low heat. Mix the softened gelatin, salad dressing, lemon juice and salt. Stir in mixed cheeses. Fold in whipped cream. Pour into eight-inch square pan or individual molds. Chill until set. May be served with assorted salad fruits. Makes nine servings.

(To aid in removing salads from mold or pan, grease mold very lightly with vegetable oil before filling is added. Dip in warm water before unmolding.)

END OF THE WEEK PIE

½ C mayonnaise
½ C milk
2 eggs, slightly beaten

1 C shredded cheese, any kind
1½ C left-over meat
½ C left-over vegetables

1 - 8 or 9 inch pie shell, unbaked

Combine well the first three ingredients and fold in remaining ingredients. Pour into pie shell and bake at 350⁰ for 40 minutes.

(Since this is a fine, quick dish to have when the larder is low, use any left-over meats that you find in your refrigerator. Turkey, chicken, pork, ham, bacon or even bologna or salami are good. Small amounts of peas, green beans, corn, squash, or limas are equally good for the vegetables.)

A Sprig from the Tree of Virtue

TURKEY TURNOVERS

2 T onion, finely chopped	⅓ C gravy, slightly thickened
¼ C celery, finely chopped	½ C carrots, finely grated
1 T butter or turkey fat	1½ C turkey, include some
½ tsp salt	skin, finely chopped

Sauté onion and celery in butter until soft, about five minutes. Add remaining ingredients and stir lightly with fork to mix well. Set aside.

Biscuit mix:

1 C all purpose flour	⅛ tsp poultry seasoning
2 tsp baking powder	⅓ C shortening
¼ tsp salt	About ⅓ C milk

Sift flour, measure and resift with baking powder, salt and seasoning. Cut in shortening with pastry cutter or two knives until consistency of corn meal. Add milk all at once and stir quickly with a fork until dough stiffens. Knead lightly and quickly on a lightly floured board eight times. Roll out to a 12-inch square, and cut into four equal squares. Place one-fourth of the filling in center of each square. Moisten edge of dough and fold over. Press edges together to seal. Prick top of each turnover in several places for steam vents. Brush tops with melted butter. Place on greased baking sheet and bake at 425° for 10 to 15 minutes, or until golden brown.

(We serve the turnovers with cream gravy. Turkey gravy or a mushroom sauce could be used also. This seems to be a favorite with the men of the family and is a great way to finish the holiday turkey when you are tired of hash.)

75

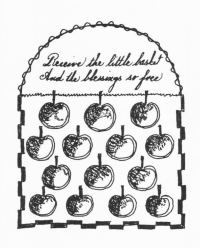

Receive the little basket
And the blessings so free

LEMON BREAD

⅓ C shortening
1 C granulated sugar
2 eggs
1½ C all purpose flour, sifted
1½ tsp baking powder

¼ tsp salt
½ C milk
grated rind of 1 lemon
½ C nuts, chopped,
  optional

Beat together shortening and sugar until light and fluffy. Add eggs, one at a time, beating well after each. Sift dry ingredients and add alternately with milk to sugar mixture, beating well after each addition. Add lemon rind and nuts if desired. Turn into one greased large loaf pan or two small ones. Bake in 350⁰ oven for about 60 minutes.

Glaze for:

⅓ C granulated sugar   juice of 1 lemon

Mix together and pour over bread immediately after removing from oven.

CRANBERRY FRUIT NUT BREAD

2 C sifted all purpose flour
1 C granulated sugar
1½ tsp baking powder
1 tsp salt
½ tsp baking soda
¼ C shortening

1 tsp grated orange peel
¾ C orange juice
1 egg, well beaten
1 C fresh cranberries,
  coarsely chopped
½ C nuts, chopped

Sift together dry ingredients. Cut in shortening. Combine peel, juice and egg; add to dry ingredients, mixing to moisten. Fold in berries and nuts. Turn into greased loaf pans and bake at 350⁰ for 60 minutes, or until done. Makes three small loaves.

BANANA BREAD

½ C butter
1 C granulated sugar
2 eggs
2 bananas, mashed

2 C all purpose flour
5 T buttermilk
½ tsp salt
1 tsp soda

Cream butter and sugar. Beat in eggs and bananas. Add one cup of the flour and half of buttermilk alternately. Add salt and soda to remaining flour. Stir in second flour mixture and remaining buttermilk alternately. Turn into well greased 9 x 5 loaf pan. Bake at 325⁰ for one hour.

SALLY LUNN BREAD

2 eggs beaten
2 T butter
1 scant C granulated
  sugar

1 C sweet milk
3 C all purpose flour
3 level tsp baking
  powder

Sift flour and baking powder together. Beat eggs. Cream butter and sugar; add milk and flour mixture alternately. Pour in eight-inch skillet. Bake at 350⁰ for 30 - 35 minutes. Score in wedges and top with dollop of butter. Serve hot.

(This is a delicious breakfast or tea bread.)

WHOLE WHEAT ROLLS

1 T dry yeast
1 C plus 1 T shortening, melted
½ C granulated sugar
1 egg

2 C lukewarm milk
1 tsp salt
3½ C wheat flour
3½ C all purpose flour

Dissolve yeast in lukewarm milk. Add egg, sugar and salt, then add whole wheat flour. Mix in shortening. Add white flour and work into ball and let rise in warm place until double in bulk. Press down, cover with towel and let rise again until double in bulk. Roll out on floured board. Pull off small balls approximately one inch in size. Place three to a cup in greased muffin tins. Brush top lightly with melted butter. Place in warm spot. Let rise until double in size. Bake at 400⁰ for 12 to 15 minutes or until brown. These freeze well to serve later.

Plumb Tree

SOUR DOUGH STARTER

For Friendship Bread

1 package dry yeast (dissolve this in ½ cup of water)
2 C all purpose flour, sifted

2 T granulated sugar
2½ C lukewarm water

Mix well all ingredients. Put in a stone crock, glass or pottery bowl and beat well. Cover with cheese cloth and let stand in a warm place for two days, until it bubbles and foams. Store in the refrigerator. Do not use a screw top cover. It can be covered with aluminum foil or similar loose fitting top.

(The night before making bread feed dough by following recipe below and then make bread according to recipe for friendship bread.)

FRIENDSHIP BREAD

(Please see starter recipe before making bread.)

2 C starter (store unused portion in refrigerator)
1½ C water
⅓ C granulated sugar
½ C cooking oil
1 T salt
4 or 5 C all purpose flour

Mix all ingredients and four cups of flour in large bowl. Empty onto floured board and knead using as much of the remaining flour as needed until you can handle the dough. Knead the dough until a hole punched in it will spring back. Put dough in a large bowl, cover with damp cloth and let rise until double in size (five to six hours). Turn out onto lightly floured board and pat out air bubbles or knead for several minutes until all air is worked out. Divide into two portions and place in greased loaf pans, 9 x 5 x 3 inches. Place in warm spot and let rise again until double in size (approximately two and one-half to three hours, since this bread rises slowly). Keep covered with a damp cloth. Place in cold oven, turn oven to 350⁰ and bake until golden brown, about 40 additional minutes. Remove from oven and while bread is still hot, butter tops of loaves freely. Turn out on rack and let cool. Bread can be reheated in foil to serve hot.

(When ready to make bread again start with "To Feed Starter".)

TO FEED STARTER

Mix with stored starter:

1½ C water
½ C granulated sugar
2 C all purpose flour, sifted

Let this sit overnight, covered lightly with a towel. This is a process called feeding and should be done every four to seven days if bread is not made. Starter must be used every two weeks to renew. If you do not wish to make bread this often, you can divide starter and give half of it to a friend to renew friendship as well as starter.

CHOCOLATE DESSERT

4 squares unsweetened
  chocolate, 4 oz
¼ C water
4 egg yolks

½ C granulated sugar
4 egg whites
dash of salt

Combine chocolate and water and melt. Cool. Beat egg yolks and sugar until pale yellow. Add cooled chocolate. Add salt to egg whites and beat until stiff peaks form. Fold egg mixture into chocolate mixture. Pour into serving dish and place in refrigerator. When ready to serve, top with whipped cream and small amount of grated chocolate.

(This is a delightful dessert treat and can be flavored with rum or coffee liqueur.)

CREAM PIE

1 C cream
1 T all purpose flour
1 C granulated sugar

2 T butter
3 egg yolks
tart jelly

Mix together flour and sugar. Cream butter with flour mixture. Add the eggs and mix. Stir in the heavy cream and pour into an unbaked pie crust. Bake at 350⁰ until set. Remove from oven and cover top of pie evenly with a thin layer of tart jelly when cool.

MERINGUE

3 egg whites
6 T granulated sugar

dash of salt

Add salt to egg whites. Beat until peaks form; then add sugar, one tablespoon at a time, beating after each addition. Continue beating until stiff and glossy, but not dry. Bake at 375⁰ until light brown, about 10 to 12 minutes.

TRANSPARENT PIE

2 C granulated sugar   4 eggs
2 T all purpose flour   ½ C cream
¾ C butter

Cream sugar and butter. Beat in eggs, flour and cream. Pour into unbaked pie shell. Bake at 350⁰ for about 45 minutes or until set.

KENTUCKY BUTTER CAKE

¾ C butter   3 tsp baking powder
1½ C granulated sugar   ¼ tsp salt
1 C milk   3 egg whites, beaten until
1 tsp vanilla   stiff
3 C all purpose flour, sifted

Sift flour, baking powder and salt together. Cream butter and sugar until very light. Add alternately flour and milk. Stir in vanilla. Fold in egg whites. Pour into two greased and lightly floured nine-inch cake pans. Bake at 350⁰ for about 30 minutes. Ice before serving.

SEVEN MINUTE FROSTING

2 egg whites   ⅛ tsp cream of tartar
1½ C granulated sugar   1 tsp vanilla
⅓ C water   dash of salt

Place water in bottom of double boiler and bring to a boil. Before placing top pan over boiling water combine in this pan all ingredients except vanilla. Beat with electric mixer. When well blended set pan over boiling water and beat mixture constantly for approximately six minutes (the power of some mixers will vary this time). Beat until mixture hangs in stiff peaks. Frequently scrape insides and bottom of double boiler with rubber spatula. Remove top pan from boiling water; add vanilla; beat until thick enough to spread, one to two minutes. Do not scrape frosting too closely from bottom of pan as frosting may sugar.

JELLY ROLL

4 eggs
¾ C cake flour, sifted
¾ tsp baking powder
¼ tsp salt

¾ C granulated sugar
1 tsp vanilla
powdered sugar
1 C tart jelly or jam

Let eggs sit at room temperature for one hour. When ready to make cake, start heating oven to 400⁰. With wax paper, line bottom of 15½ x 10½ inch jelly roll pan. Sift together flour, baking powder and salt. In small bowl, with electric mixer at high speed, beat eggs until foamy. Beat rapidly, adding sugar slowly. Continue beating until very thick and light colored. With rubber spatula or spoon, fold in flour mixture and vanilla. Turn into pan, spreading batter evenly. Bake 13 minutes or until light brown. Lightly dust clean tea towel or waxed paper with powdered sugar. When cake is done, loosen it from sides of pan. Invert onto towel. Lift off pan and carefully peel off paper. With very sharp knife, cut crisp edges from cake. Spread cake with jam or jelly to within half an inch of edges. Start rolling up cake from narrow end by folding edge of cake over then tucking it under, continue rolling cake, lifting the towel higher and higher with one hand as you guide roll with the other. Finish with open end of cake on bottom. Wrap towel tightly around roll to shape it. Finish cooling on rack and sprinkle with powdered sugar again.

LEMON SAUCE

½ C granulated sugar
1 T corn starch
1½ tsp lemon juice
1 tsp lemon rind

2 T butter
1 C boiling water
a few grains of salt

Mix sugar and corn starch. Gradually add boiling water. Boil five minutes. Remove from heat and add other ingredients. Serve the sauce hot on sliced jelly roll.

OATMEAL COOKIES WITH BUTTERSCOTCH

¾ C shortening
1 C brown sugar
½ C granulated sugar
1 egg
¼ C water
1 tsp vanilla
1 C all purpose flour

½ tsp soda
1 tsp salt
2 C quick rolled oats,
   uncooked
1 - 6 oz package butterscotch
   morsels

Cream shortening and sugars. Blend in egg, water and vanilla; mixing well. Sift together flour, soda and salt. Add this to shortening mixture and blend well. Stir in oats. Add butterscotch morsels. Drop by teaspoons onto a greased cookie sheet. Bake at 350° for 12 to 15 minutes. Makes seven to eight dozen cookies.

COCONUT BARS

1 C sifted all purpose flour
¼ C firmly-packed brown sugar

½ C soft butter

Combine flour and sugar. Add butter and mix until thoroughly blended. Batter will be stiff and sticky. Smooth batter out in bottom of a greased eight inch square pan. Bake at 350° for 15 to 20 minutes.

2 eggs
1 C firmly packed brown sugar
¼ C sifted all purpose flour

½ tsp baking powder
1 tsp vanilla
1½ C shredded coconut

Beat eggs until light and foamy. Add sugar gradually, beating constantly until mixture is light and fluffy. Sift flour with the baking powder. Beat flour mixture into egg mixture. Add vanilla and coconut. Mix well. Spread on top of baked mixture. Return to oven. Bake 20 to 25 minutes or until lightly browned. Score top in squares and cool at least one hour before cutting into bars. Makes about 24 bars.

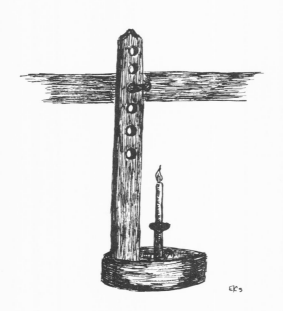

Index

A star beside a recipe indicates that this is the proper name. Recipes are also listed under general headings, such as Beverages or Soups.

88

If you would like additional copies of this book or you would like to order the first cookbook, We Make You Kindly Welcome, please write:

Shakertown Inc.
Route 4
Harrodsburg, Kentucky 40330